Praise for Sink or Swim

I truly couldn't put down this book of the amazing true story of Karin Rooney. Her transparency with the challenges she endured and the victories over them is truly inspiring as she shares with her readers about her and her husband's flight as passengers on Captain Sully's plane that he crash-landed into the freezing Hudson River.

I highly recommend this book for teenagers, single young adults, married adults, and grandparents. It will increase your faith and strengthen your resolve that we can face any hardship that comes our way through God's Grace and his ability to stay near us and help us in times of trouble.

As a trauma specialist, I recommend all workers in our field to read this book and gain raw, real, and relevant insight into a person who has endured a rare incident of trauma, and searched for healing and wholeness after surviving the unthinkable.

—Victor Marx,
Founder and President,
All Things Possible (ATP) Ministries

SINK or SWIM

Life After Crash Landing in the Hudson

BY

KARIN ROONEY

WITH JESSIE M. SANTALA

Deep River
B O O K S

Karin's Dedication

To Kalyn Elizabeth Peterson and Roman Jesse Ferra. Your lives
have been a light to me.

Jessie's Dedication

For the loves of my life—Mike, Charlotte and Felix.

Acknowledgments

Karin's Acknowledgments

This book would not have been possible without Captain Chesley "Sully" Sullenberger and the entire flight crew from US Airways Flight 1549, and if Jessie Santala and Deep River Books had not believed in my story of life after the crash landing on the Hudson River. I would like to express my deepest gratitude to all the wonderful people who helped make this book possible.

Thank you, Chris; you'll always be my #1.

To my kids, Big Heart, Middle Heart and Little Heart: You've helped me conquer my fears.

To my mom and dad: I cannot thank you enough for raising me to know where true hope comes from. Daily you offer me encouragement and I'm so grateful for both of you.

To my family and friends: Thank you for all your love and support.

Denise, Dawn and Patricia: You have held me to the fire of truth and given me strength to keep seeing God's goodness.

Above all, to the One who truly saved me and gave me new hope and new life.

Jessie's Acknowledgments

Through this process, I have learned so much about God's faithfulness, His provision and His perfect timing. To Him be the glory.

Karin, I am humbled that you trusted me to help tell your story. Thank you.

To the staff at Deep River Books, thank you for taking a chance on us and for guiding us along the way.

Mikey, your belief in me kept me going even when I doubted. And I'm not just talking about this book. You are a gift.

Charlotte and Felix, what a joy to be your mommy! I love you both so much.

Daddy and Mama, you taught me to read and to love the written word. You also taught me to trust Jesus and love people. This wouldn't have happened without you.

To my sisters, Bethany and Gwendolyn and my niece, Dakota; I am glad that Jesus made us both family and friends.

Shannon, you know all too well that life can change in an instant and nothing is guaranteed. You also know that God is good, no matter what. Thank you for your support, your encouragement and for having the courage to share your faith with honesty. #LoveWithNoRegrets

And for Quiche. Because you are the unicorn of people.

Contents

Preface

No doubt people will debate whether there is life after death until the world ends. Even those of us who believe in the existence of eternal life aren't in any hurry to verify it through personal experience.

Ann Spangler[1]

There is an old story about a man who, when teaching his son how to swim, decided that the best method was to simply throw his son into the water and see how he responded. He thought that his son would learn best by complete immersion and that in his desperate need to avoid sinking, he would learn to swim.

To some people, the father's methods may seem cruel, but I can relate to that story. I learn best when I get to experience life through full immersion. I don't just want to read a book about a place or a concept or an idea. I want to be there. I want to experience it. I want to soak it in.

I also want to be in control.

This affinity for real-life experiences can be both a blessing and a hardship. It can lead to experiencing both the bad and the good that life has to offer.

I was at a point in my life where I felt a bit stalled and I didn't like it one bit. I have always been a bit of a control freak and feeling like I was just treading water in life wasn't sitting well with me. I was at a standstill when it came to love, looking for a change in my most significant relationship. I was questioning what I wanted to do with my life and was contemplating a change in my college major. I was also going deeper in my faith, something that I had wrestled with in the past. I am not afraid of change, especially when it is necessary—and it felt necessary. I felt like I was on the brink of something big, important, life-changing, but didn't know how to go about moving forward. I needed to be challenged.

I wasn't looking for a complete upheaval in my life, but then again, who is? God sensed my needs and sent change knocking on my door in the most unusual of ways. He sent me down a unique, and to be honest, quite frightening path. It was full immersion to the greatest extent. I even got wet.

It was a lonely path, one that not many people could understand, but it was the path that God chose to set my feet upon and I haven't looked back. My experience is a unique one, but the lessons I learned along the way are ones that most people can relate to and my experiences are ones that I wouldn't change. This is the story of my journey and how, when I was overwhelmed with my circumstances and felt like I was sinking, I learned to swim.

SECTION ONE

Crashing

My whole life, experiences are proof of the sovereignty of God and his direct interference in the lives of men. I cannot help believing what I believe. I would be a madman to believe anything else—the guiding hand of God!

Dr. Martyn Lloyd-Jones[2]

1

Brace for Impact

I have always been a bit of a nervous flyer. There's something about not fully understanding how airplanes get up and stay in the air that makes me hesitant to climb into those giant metal "birds." My nerves also stem from my lack of control. I have no power to determine whether or not we stay in the air and that makes me incredibly uncomfortable.

Now I have an excuse for my nerves and a pretty good one at that. Back in 2009, I didn't have an excuse, but that didn't stop me from feeling nervous anyway.

The morning had been fun and had seemed like the perfect ending to our first trip as a couple. New York City had lived up to its hype and the trip had gone better than I had anticipated. I was leaving New York feeling hopeful about my relationship with Chris, something that I hadn't felt in a while. As we rode the bus to the airport though, I could feel some of my old concerns about our relationship welling up inside, and I quickly pushed the emotions away.

At the airport with time to kill, we walked past a spa and I debated about whether or not I should treat myself before boarding the plane.

"Babe, should I get a pedicure?" I ask Chris, stopping in front of the store, making his long legs come to a halt. It had been a long week of walking in New York. I had bought new boots just for this trip and although they were cute, they hadn't been broken in yet which had caused me considerable pain as we walked the streets of New York. I was in the mood for some pampering before our long flight home to Colorado. I wouldn't classify myself as superficial, but I did have a love of fashion and an appreciation for small indulgences like pedicures.

"It's expensive. But my calves hurt from walking around in boots this week and it would be so nice to be relaxed before I get on the plane," I said, flashing him a grin.

"You don't need a pedicure," Chris said, rolling his eyes a little and starting to walk away. Always realistic, Chris had little interest in pampering for himself or anyone else.

I stood there for a moment debating on whether or not I agreed before regretfully following Chris to our gate.

We barely had situated ourselves in the waiting area when we heard the boarding call over the intercom. When the flight attendant called our boarding group I stood and got in line immediately, which is unusual for me. I always had a system that I followed when flying, and it didn't include boarding early. I have always disliked waiting in any line, especially waiting in line to board an airplane. I hate getting bumped by other passengers' carry-on luggage as I board and I get impatient having to stand in the crowded aisle while people put their baggage away. I also don't like standing in the breezeway that leads to the plane. It makes me feel edgy. When I have flown in the past I have always waited until the last second to board, but for some reason on this day I veered from my usual routine. Just as I suspected, there was a big, slow moving line.

"This is why I don't board right away," I muttered as I stood in the narrow aisle waiting for another passenger to cram his bag into the already crowded overhead bin. We had checked our bags and I was grateful not to have to try to find room for a carry-on, since there didn't appear to be any left.

I overheard one of the flight attendants say "The plane is full," and I could feel my tension grow.

How will the plane fly if it's full? I wondered. A guy boarding the plane in front of me had a giant piece of art wrapped in plain brown paper. He was awkwardly trying to navigate the aisle without injuring the art or his fellow passengers. The plane was so full that he asked if he could put it in the cargo hold of the plane. I had no idea how it was going to be safe there.

I hope his art makes it, I thought as I continued to file down the center aisle.

We finally made our way to row 18, eight rows back from the wings, and settled into our seats. "Chris, say a prayer for our trip," I half asked, half demanded. I always make a point of praying before leaving on a trip, something that had been instilled in me by my parents. Before my family set out on any of the many road trips we took when I was a kid, we would always take a moment to pray for "traveling safeties."

"Sure," Chris said, taking my hand and bowing his head. "Lord, we thank you that we had such a great time in New York and we ask that you please keep us safe on the way back to Colorado. Amen."

"Amen," I echoed.

As soon as he finished, my mouth went wild, words jumping over each other in their attempt to get out first. I chattered to Chris and to the poor man who had been given the seat next to me. I could hear the quickness in my voice and I knew that it was an attempt to alleviate some of the apprehension I always felt about flying. I had never been given any reason to fear flying beyond a bit of turbulence a time or two, but the whole process still unnerved me.

"How do planes fly, Chris? I mean, how does something so big stay in the air?" I ask him, eager to fill the silence that had settled over the plane as we begin taxiing down the runway. With a degree in engineering physics from the University of Colorado and a pilot for a father, I knew that Chris would have the answer.

"The air goes over and under the wing and creates a lift," Chris patiently explained, demonstrating with his hands as we taxied down the runway. He could tell that I was nervous.

I could feel the plane leave the ground and as the plane rose higher and higher, I began to relax. I had just settled back into my seat, only half listening to Chris's explanation when I heard The Noise and felt the plane shake.

"Oh my gosh, Chris, what was that?" I ask, sitting up with a jolt. I can hear the nervous whispers of the other passengers around me, which does nothing to calm my nerves.

"It's OK, Karin. It's OK," he says soothingly, but his face looks stressed. (He will later tell me that he immediately knew that things were not all right, but in that moment he was trying to keep me from panicking, something that I was already on the verge of doing.) Something has gone horribly wrong. I can feel it in my gut, but in the moment I am desperate to believe him and so I pretend that he is right. We're OK.

The noise is jarring, but not as jarring as the fact that it is immediately followed by a 180-degree turn of the plane. I can hear the other passengers around me turn their whispers into louder, more concerned murmurs. Uneasiness rises in my chest and I am heavy with an overwhelming sense of needing to pray, not only on behalf of our plane, but also in an attempt to stay calm.

"God, protect our plane," I say, putting my hand up and leaning forward in my seat. I don't care what other passengers think of my posture or my prayer. "Gently lay our plane down. Put your angels above, below, in front and behind our plane. Lay this plane down gently." I repeat it a few times.

My words strike me as odd and yet, I can't stop praying them over and over again. I have no time to question exactly why I would pray such a specific prayer. I feel the plane turning about in the air and I hear a baby start to cry somewhere in the plane. I squeeze Chris's hand tight and look at him, hoping to find some kind of reassurance. He looks at me and I see the fear in his eyes. My stomach drops before bouncing back up and into my mouth.

We're just going back to the airport, I tell myself to keep the rising panic down. *We're just going back to the airport where we'll land and they'll fix whatever is wrong with the plane. Just keep praying, Karin, and things will be all right.*

A voice on the intercom interrupts me.

"Ladies and Gentlemen, this is your captain. Brace for impact."

At his announcement, the flight attendants begin chanting "Brace, brace, brace," in eerie unison from their stations around the plane. I don't exactly know what it means to brace, but I know that it isn't good.

OK, we're in for a rough landing at the airport. You're going to be all right, Karin, I tell myself again, but I am a horrible liar. I don't believe a word I am saying and yet I keep telling myself, *You and Chris are going to be fine.*

I don't know how to brace myself. For the first time in my life, I wish that I had paid attention to the flight attendant's presentation before the flight took off. I had brushed it off thinking, *Nothing's going to happen. It's just precautionary.* Yet now I find myself wondering what I should be doing. I peek around at the other passengers and see people bending forward in their seats with their arms in various positions. Some are covering their heads; some are literally bracing themselves on the seats in front of them.

"I love you, Chris," I say, kissing him gently before I curl over into his lap. I know it probably isn't the right way to brace, but it feels the safest to me. Besides, I want to be as close to the man that I love as possible when whatever is coming happens.

"I love you too," I hear him whisper into my hair as he wraps his arms around me. The plane falls eerily silent as we brace and wait for the inevitable. We are going to crash.

2

Some Background

My name is Karin Rooney and I am the survivor of a plane crash. Chances are you don't know me or recognize my name, but you've probably heard my story. You see, I was on US Airways Flight 1549 in January of 2009, the flight that crashed into the Hudson River on a cold winter's day. I am one of the 155 survivors and I am part of what was later dubbed the "Miracle on the Hudson." I am one of the people who stood on the wing of the plane and waited to be rescued and I am one of the people whose life was forever changed by that event. I am a survivor, a member of a small group of people who can say that they walked away from a plane crash. But my story doesn't start or, thanks to God's grace, end there. That's just a small part of it, an event in my life. I'm here to tell you the rest of my story and how this one event started me down a road of faith-building and self-discovery.

Back in 2009, I was still Karin Hill, a young college student looking forward to taking a trip to New York with my then-boyfriend, Chris Rooney. We were traveling with a couple of Chris's guy friends to see some of our friends who lived in New York. The guys were planning some activities and I was going to spend time with my friend Anna. It was an important trip to both of us, not just because it was our first official trip as a couple, but also because it had the potential to be our only trip as a couple.

Our two-year relationship had gotten off to a slow start. In 2004, both Chris and I were going to Campus Crusade (now called Cru), a college ministry at the University of Colorado in Boulder, Colorado. We were also both in a college ministry called the Annex that was sponsored by a local Boulder church. It was our freshman year and since arriving on campus, I had done my best to meet as many people as I could. I was a self-proclaimed social butterfly and I liked it that way. Many of the people that I met were nice, but didn't really stand out in my memory. Chris was different.

The first thought that crossed my mind the night that I met Chris was, *Oh my goodness. He's so good-looking.* It was quickly followed by, *You have to get to know this guy.*

He didn't make any real effort to get to know me and so I decided to take matters into my own hands after being introduced.

"What are you doing this summer?" I asked him after a church service.

"Painting."

"Houses? Cool. I'm going to Oregon for the summer. To see my family. I'll be babysitting my cousin all summer and I'll probably try to get a part-time job, maybe waiting tables or something. Maybe get my email so we can keep in touch?"

I could hear myself babbling, but I couldn't seem to stop.

"Sure," he said before giving me his email address and walking away.

During my time in Oregon I emailed Chris exactly once. It was a simple email saying hi, telling him about my summer in Oregon and probably saying "hope to see you in the fall." I never heard from him and so I didn't reach out to him again. When I got home I pushed him from my mind.

By my sophomore year, I had all but forgotten about Chris. When I returned from Oregon I felt disconnected from the

Annex and from my friends, too. Most of them had stayed in Colorado and had grown close over the summer. I still attended meetings at the Annex, but Chris was more involved with Campus Crusade so we didn't see each other often, which was fine with me. Although we would run across each other occasionally, nothing came of it. Every time I saw him, I felt that same thrill, but he didn't seem interested and so I didn't pursue anything. I put him out of my head.

In December, I decided last minute that I was going to go to a Denver Christmas Conference with some of the students involved with Campus Crusade. I wasn't connected with anyone, I just needed something to do and it sounded fun. The day after New Year's Eve we all bundled up, piled into some cars and drove to Denver from Boulder. I didn't really know anyone, except my sister and her boyfriend, and they had their own friends they were meeting up with. This had caused me to feel hesitant at first, but as we began to drive to Denver, I felt an excitement begin to build in me, a sense of anticipation.

I had settled into my room and was walking through the hotel to head to my first meeting when I saw Chris. I felt my throat tighten and my stomach fill with nerves. I hadn't expected to see him here and I really hadn't expected my body to react so strongly to the sight of him. I didn't want to see him and yet, I couldn't get away.

"Hi," I heard a voice say and I immediately recognized it as his.

"Hi," I said, feeling uncharacteristically shy.

"Going in?" He asked, pointing to the meeting room.

"Yep."

"Mind if I sit with you?"

"Sure," I said walking through the door he held open for me. "I didn't think you'd be here. It's nice to see you."

"It's nice to see you too," he said with a smile and I felt my heart jump in my chest.

We spent most of our time together that week. When it was time to go, I realized that I was sold. I had found the man that I wanted to spend the rest of my life with. Did he feel the same way? I just couldn't tell.

When we got back to Boulder after the conference, things changed. He asked me on a date and I readily agreed to go. We saw *Hitch* and got ice cream and had a wonderful time together, or so I thought. I waited for him to call and ask me out again. He didn't. Eight weeks later, he still hadn't said anything about going out again and I didn't know what to think.

"Are you going to ask me out on another date?" I asked him one day, getting right to the point. I have never been one to beat around the bush. I like to speak my mind.

Chris sighed, "I'm not interested in you like that."

"OK. I like you. I think you know that. But I also like you as a friend and I don't want things to get weird. I'm all right being just friends if that's what you want," I said and I saw relief pass over his face. I was interested in him. No, I was more than interested. I thought I could marry him, but I also really liked being his friend and I didn't want to jeopardize that. Chris had so many of the qualities I was hoping for in a husband: He was a Christian; he had a good sense of humor; he enjoyed having fun and he cared very much for his family and friends. I couldn't stop thinking about him and hoping that something would change, but he seemed content to be just friends and eventually I realized that I needed to move on.

My friends set me up on a blind date and somehow the news made it back to Chris. I'll never know how, but within two weeks he had asked me out again. I said yes without hesitation and we began dating.

He told me that he wanted to exclusively date me. Within five months he had told me that he loved me and I was thrilled. I began to imagine our life together as man and wife because everyone knows you don't just tell a girl you love her without being serious.

3

New York, New York

In the beginning, our relationship was wonderful just as most relationships are. After months of wanting to be with Chris, I could barely believe that my desire had actually come true. I loved every minute that we spent together and I could hardly stand to be apart. I wanted to know everything about him and the sight of him still made my heart jump.

We were planning a trip to New York and what should have been an exciting time was quickly turning into something less than joyful. Our relationship had turned tense over the past few months because we seemed to have different relationship goals. I knew where I wanted our relationship to go, but Chris seemed to be dragging his feet and I couldn't understand why. Although we never verbalized it to each other, we both knew deep down that this trip to New York was going to be an important step in our relationship. It had the power to decide whether we moved on together or went our separate ways.

"I love you, Karin," he would frequently tell me. "But, I'm just not ready to marry you."

"I love you too, Chris and I want to marry you," I would answer. "I don't understand why you're not ready."

His declarations of love were both reassuring and frustrating. He loved me. He didn't want to marry me, at least at that time. I loved him. To me, it made perfect sense that Chris and I would get married. After all, we had been dating for quite some time and besides, I *really, really* liked him. I had known him as a friend and I had known him as a boyfriend and I loved both aspects of our relationship. Now, I wanted to know him as my husband.

It was easy for me to visualize being married to him and I couldn't understand why he couldn't visualize it too. I loved the fact that he was so close to his family. Every weekend he would go home for birthdays. He wasn't fickle. He had friends that he had known and loved for years. I wanted to move forward in our relationship, which in my mind meant marriage, and yet, he seemed to be in no rush to commit to me. He wasn't running away, but he definitely wasn't moving forward either and I was frustrated. I didn't need a marriage proposal right now, but I did need some kind of sign that I wasn't wasting my time with Chris, and that was something that he was either unable or unwilling to give.

I had been praying for months that God would do something in Chris's life that would cause him to make a decision about me. I knew that I wouldn't have the strength to leave Chris on my own, but neither did I have the patience to sit and wait for him to make up his mind about whether or not he was going to marry me. I needed Chris to move out of his current state of comfort with our relationship and either decide to commit or get out. I should have been more specific in my prayers, but I wasn't. I simply left it up to God to do what He would. And man, did He!

As our plane took off from Denver International Airport I thought about what this trip could mean for our future. I was hoping that this trip would be a catalyst of some kind; that it would show Chris how much fun we had together and how much we liked each other. I wanted the trip to solidify in some way that we were good together. We had never traveled together and I knew that travel can sometimes be stressful and crazy and I hoped that the stress would bring us closer together rather than pushing us apart.

As soon as we got close enough to New York to see anything, I glued my face to the window of the plane. I just couldn't seem to take enough of it in. It was so exciting to see in real life the landmarks that I had heard about and seen only in pictures. I saw the Statue of Liberty and was so thrilled I could barely stay in my seat.

"Look, Chris. Look!" I kept saying, pointing to things through the tiny oval window oblivious to the fact that he could probably see nothing past the back of my head. I turned to look at him and saw that he was smiling at me, obviously delighted with my excitement. I felt a surge of love for him.

God, do something in Chris's heart on this trip that helps him decide how he feels about our relationship, I quickly prayed as we began our descent into New York.

I had always believed in God, but my faith had had its ups and downs. In the past few months, though, I had developed a hunger to know God more intimately, to experience His faithfulness in tangible ways and to increase in my faith. My prayer had been to know God better and to trust Him more and I had prayed it over and over again without ever getting a sense that He was moving in my life. It felt frustrating to be praying so many prayers without response and yet, I believed that God would answer them. I just needed to be patient, which I wasn't very good at doing.

Be careful what you pray for. We serve a powerful God who answers prayers in unexpected ways.

4

Control Issues

As I have mentioned, I have struggled with control for much of my life and I think it started fairly innocently. My need for control wasn't something I consciously thought about, but rather something that grew because of circumstances in my life.

Some of my childhood experiences left me with a strong desire to control my life in order to prevent painful experiences. I made up my mind that I wouldn't let anything bad happen to me again and the best way that I knew how to do this was to try and anticipate what the future held and develop a plan.

I became a planner. A good one.

I planned my outfits. I planned my meals. I planned my work schedule. I planned my class schedule. And most of all, I planned my relationship with Chris.

I planned so that I wouldn't have to experience any more traumas in my life.

The morning of December 15 I planned to fly back home to Colorado. I was trying not to think about what would happen with our relationship when we landed. We had just had an amazing trip and I was thankful for the chance to take this time to just be together and explore the world together. I also felt quite proud of myself. My plan to prove that I would be excellent wife material on this trip seemed to have worked. I just hoped that Chris had seen it.

5

A Wing and a Prayer

We are crashing and I think that everyone on the plane knows but me. I don't allow the words *plane crash* to pass through my mind, though, because that would be too much to handle. The optimism that I have relied on my entire life doesn't fail me; although I know our plane is in trouble, I refuse to allow myself to think about what the consequences might be.

I don't look out the window, even though I am sitting in the window seat. I don't want to. If you know your plane is having problems, it seems like the right thing to do to look outside for what might be your last glimpse of life, but I don't. I have already convinced myself that we are merely making an emergency landing at the airport and that we will land safely, have a drink to calm our nerves, laugh about how scared we all were, change planes and be on our way again. I know that I will be in Colorado tonight, a littler later than we planned, but we will make it.

If I had looked out of the window, I would have known exactly how wrong I was.

To this day I can't give you any reason why I didn't look out the window except that God must have been protecting me. If I would have known that we were landing on the water, I don't know what I would have done or how I would have reacted. I think the knowledge would have paralyzed me during a time when action was required. Chris knew what was happening. He could see out the window and he would later tell me that he was sure that we were going to die.

Bracing for the moment of impact as the flight attendants had instructed, I knew that we were in for a bumpy landing, but had no idea the gravity of the situation. The actual moment of impact slips from my memory because everything that followed happened so fast. I remember the jolt of landing and then I remembering sitting up.

"We're OK. We're at the airport," I whisper to myself. I turn to look around only to find water rushing into the cabin. I immediately panic as the reality of what has just happened begins to sink it.

"Oh, my God! Oh, my God. Chris!" I scream, but he doesn't answer. I feel him reaching across me and unbuckling my seatbelt and then ripping me out of my seat. My mind begins to work overtime trying to piece together what is happening. *We're in the water. We're going to drown. That's what happens in the movies when you're in water. I should probably grab my purse. Wait, I can't grab my purse. It's too late. We're going to drown in the cabin of the airplane.*

People begin climbing over the rows of seats, while others start filing down the aisle as if we were exiting after a normal flight. I see someone grab his seat cushion and I make a desperate grab for mine even as Chris is hustling me down the aisle. I don't know what a seat cushion could do to help us, but it seems like a good thing to do. For the second time in a few short minutes I wish to God I had listened to the flight attendant's safety speech. As I look back toward the tail of the plane, I see people standing in water up to their necks and a fresh wave of panic washes over me.

Our seats are eight rows back from the wing exit. Thankfully, I *had* located the exit nearest to me at the beginning of our flight. I don't know where I am going or what I am supposed to be doing, I just know that Chris is in front of me and that I have to stay with Chris. Suddenly, someone cuts in front of me in the aisle separating me from Chris and any peace that I have left flies away.

"Chris, don't leave me!" I scream, feeling my body becoming paralyzed with panic. He turns and heads back toward me. People push past him in a hurry until I finally reach him again. He puts me in front of him and steers me by my shoulders out of the airplane and onto the wing. Before I know it we are standing in a crowd of passengers on the wing, looking out over the Hudson River. It is bitterly cold.

The details of the moments between impact and exit remain very clear in my mind, but from the time we got safely onto the wing, my memories get a little fuzzy. Blame my panic or the fact that I felt as though we were standing there for hours . . . I don't know. My memories of standing there on the wing, waiting for whatever was going to happen next, come in bits and pieces, but those bits are as clear as photographs to me.

I remember how the ice forming on my clothes scratched me and I didn't like it. I remember throwing my hat and scarf into the Hudson because they were getting heavy with ice. I don't remember feeling too cold, even though I know I was.

I remember being glad that I had waterproofed my new boots before coming on the trip, even as the water was rising up to my chest. Fashion was out the window, literally, but I was still thankful my boots were protected.

I remember briefly entertaining the thought of whether or not I could keep myself afloat long enough to be rescued if it came to that.

I remember the sense of relief I felt when I saw the ferryboats approaching us. I remember calling out that everything would be OK, with the idea of giving people hope when in reality I needed hope for myself. I remember Chris telling me to stop yelling.

And I remember hearing God's voice as I prayed and watched Chris help other passengers climb to safety telling me that Chris was a good man who was worth the wait. It is an odd time to be thinking about marriage, but what better time to hear God's voice than in the middle of a crisis?

A sense of peace rushed over me even as people were scrambling to safety around me. I felt calm settle in my soul. I clung to those words: *Chris is worth the wait,* and I repeated them over and over to myself even as people talked around me. I understood that I needed to be patient and that Chris would propose to me in God's time. God's words preoccupied my mind, even as I was rescued by a ferryboat. Those words kept me feeling peaceful all the way back to shore.

6

Rescued

We are grateful to be rescued but the ferries have one flaw: You have to climb a ladder to board, which is nearly impossible since we are soaking wet and freezing cold. The ladders shake and lurch with every tilt of the boat making the climb even more dangerous. The water that was up to our ankles when we first exited onto the wing is now up to our necks. Chris starts helping people around us exit the wing and climb to safety. While we are not safe yet, it feels reassuring to see our plane surrounded by ferryboats, the Coast Guard and other boats that have come to assist.

Chris and I end up being rescued by different teams of people. Chris is rescued by a fishing boat and I am rescued by the Coast Guard, and this causes me to be freshly awash with panic. Losing sight of him as his rescue boat pulls away from mine is gut-wrenchingly awful. We have just been through the most traumatic experience of our lives, and the last thing I want is to be separated from him.

Looking back, however, I can see what God was doing. It was good to be separated because it gave us some time to think about each other and what we had just been through. I later learned that they took Chris to the hospital to be checked for hypothermia while I was taken to a restaurant that had been closed in order to take care of the plane-crash survivors. He told me that our time apart helped solidify in his heart the fact that I was "the one" for him. Even as we were recovering from the shock of our ordeal, God was working.

As I walked through the door of the restaurant with a herd of other rescued passengers, friendly people and a flurry of activity greeted me. Someone handed me a ball of white fabric while someone else asked me questions about who I was and where I came from. These people then proceeded to tag me like a piece of luggage. I looked down at the fabric in my hands in a daze, barely listening to the people directing questions my way. When I realized that I was holding a tablecloth I laughed out loud. The words, "change into this" come floating back and I knew that I was supposed to change out of my wet clothes into a tablecloth. The thought of all of these passengers walking around in tablecloth togas made me smile. I shook my head at how painstakingly I had planned out my airplane outfit only to have lost part of it in the Hudson and then to find myself walking around in my underwear and a sheet later on that day. A pedicure seemed frivolous and I wondered why I even wanted one. I wondered if I was the same person.

From my spot in the restaurant I had a direct view of the Hudson River. I stood and watched as the plane slowly sank into the water. I knew that I was just on that plane. I had the snapshots in my mind of the crash, but my mind didn't seem willing or able to fully accept what had just happened.

I assess how I am feeling. Surprisingly, I find that I don't feel scared. I don't feel relief either. I just feel nothing; a numbness seeps into every crack of my being; everything around me seems surreal. "Oh, my gosh. This is insane. That was us?" I say out loud to no one in particular. I stare at the river and yet I can't wrap my mind around the fact that I have just been in a plane crash.

People keep asking me if I am all right and I don't know how to respond. Am I all right? It only happened, like, five minutes ago so I don't know how I am. The reality of the situation hits me as vaguely humorous. I was in a plane crash and now here I am, wrapped in a tablecloth.

From a corner of the restaurant, a woman starts singing. I listen to the words and I realize that she is singing a hymn. I slowly make my way over to her, seeming to float on the words of her song. "Excuse me. Do you believe in God?" I ask when she has finished.

"Yeah, that was the work of the Lord," she replies. Tears spring to my eyes, the tears that I had been without all afternoon, and the reality of what we have just been through slowly starts to sink in. She looks at me and I can see her eyes filling with tears as well. I feel inspired and uplifted seeing someone praise God after what we have just endured.

The sound of crying echoes around the restaurant and I realize that I am not alone in my tears. There isn't an overwhelming sound of sobbing, just a quiet sense of pain in people's voices. Other people are laughing, in a seeming state of euphoria because we have defied all odds and survived. That is a weird mingling of sounds of joy, relief and pain.

In that moment, it becomes incredibly clear to me how blessed I am to have Chris. Some of the people traveling today are alone, but I'm not. I had someone to whom to say, "I will look at you, you will look at me and we will be strong for each other" while the plane was going down. Not everyone had that comfort. Some people are alone and they are scared and worried and without the comfort of having someone they love nearby. Having Chris with me, even though we are apart at the moment and in fact I don't know where he is, changes how I respond. I don't feel alone. I know that the one I love most is safe somewhere and is probably looking for me already. That is all that matters at this moment in time.

7

Reunited

The first responders have found a more suitable place for the passengers to stay while they account for all passengers. We are moved from the restaurant to another location, a place called The Nutrition Center down the street. Once we arrive a volunteer comes to check on me, and for the first time I realize that our crash must have been in the news.

"Do you have a phone I could borrow?" I ask, wondering if my parents are worried or if they have even heard. She hands me her cell phone and with shaky hands I dial my dad's number in Louisville, Colorado. He doesn't pick up. (He will tell me later that he didn't recognize the number.) I proceed to leave him a message; a confusing jumble of words and emotions.

"Dad, we were in a plane crash, we're all right. We were in the water. The Coast Guard got me. The water was up to my chest, but we're all right."

He said that when he listened to the message, he initially thought that I had merely seen a plane crash and had become afraid to fly, but after listening to me go on and on about water and the Coast Guard he realized what I was saying. His immediate response was to drive to the downtown Louisville library where my mom and older sister were spending the day.

"Cathy," he said after frantically combing the aisles of the library for my mom. "Karin and Chris are all right, but they were in a plane crash." Mom's face registered her shock and she went searching through the library to find my sister.

"Karin and Chris were in a plane crash," she blurted out as soon as she saw Sarah, my older sister. In her haste, she forgot to add "they're all right," and my sister later told me that, for a brief moment, she thought I had died.

I keep trying to call home every chance I got, and when at last I am able to talk to my dad in person, I feel myself starting to break down. I try to tell him the facts, but they don't come out much clearer than the first message. I hear tears in my voice and I know that, despite my words, I am doing a horrible job convincing him that I am all right.

Second on my list of priorities, after contacting my parents, is to find Chris. We have been separated for several hours and I am anxious to be reunited. I don't know how to go about this process.

"I need to find my boyfriend. He was on the plane. I know a ferry picked him up and I don't know where he is. Where could he be?" I start asking anyone who will listen. When a group of detectives arrives to interview all surviving passengers, I ask them if they know where other passengers have been taken.

"We don't know, but we'll certainly try to find him," one of them assures me.

After 9/11 I had heard many people on the news and in the newspapers praise the New York and New Jersey police officers and first responders. And now I am getting to experience first-hand their kindness and willingness to help. Everything that I read is true. The Red Cross volunteers have been working over-time to clean and dry our soaked clothes and have gone out of their way to make sure that we each have whatever we need. They have a big screen television set up for us to watch and we all take turns stopping and staring at ourselves on the news. It is strange to be surrounded by over a hundred people who you don't know and yet are going out of their way to help you.

"We're looking for Karin Hill," a police officer announces to the room.

"I'm Karin Hill," I say jumping up, my heart pounding.

"We're going to take you."

"Who's taking me? Where are you taking me?" I ask quickly.

"We heard you're looking for Chris. We're taking you to him at the hospital."

My heart starts pounding even harder at the word "hospital." When I had last seen Chris he had seemed fine. Had something happened in between us being rescued and now? The police officers quickly assure me that Chris is fine and tell me that he had been taken to the hospital to ensure that he didn't have hypothermia.

"They are keeping him for observation, but everything seems fine," someone says, eager to ease my concerns.

At the hospital a nurse leads me to Chris's room. I see him sitting up in his hospital bed in a room with three other people who had been on our flight. I don't cry as I expected to. I just stand there, staring at him, because I don't know what else to do. I have never been in a situation like this before. I have not prepared for this.

"Karin," I hear his voice call out. I woodenly walk to him. When I reach his bed, I lean over to hug him. I feel such relief at seeing him again.

"Are you OK? I'm OK," I keep repeating over and over again. He holds out his hand and I put my small hand in his and I realize that I don't want to let go ever again.

"They think I have hypothermia, a low case," he says.

"Are you OK?" I ask again because I can't think of anything else to say.

I had been given some pizza and I had brought it with me and I begin passing out pieces to the people in Chris's room. We all start eating pizza and drinking the ginger ale that the hospital has provided. Neither Chris nor I say a lot to each other. We don't seem to have the words to say. We have yet to process that we were in a plane crash and it strikes me as funny that after nearly dying we are doing something as mundane as eating pizza and drinking soda.

Suddenly, the doctor walks in and I can feel my body stiffen.

"You're good to go, Chris," he says with little introduction and I hear myself sigh in relief. "Call me tomorrow if you're not feeling well."

And with that, we are on our way.

8

Recovery

The next few hours are a whirlwind. We are driven to the Crown Plaza Hotel with four other people from our flight. Once there, US Airways gives us clothes and packages full of toiletries.

At the hotel we are all escorted into a large conference room filled with small tables. We are led to a table where volunteers from the Red Cross were waiting for us.

"How are you doing?" One of the volunteers asks me.

Abruptly, the tears that had been missing when I had been reunited with Chris start rolling down my cheeks. I am touched by how kind these people who don't know me from Adam have been to me during the worst hours of my life. Embarrassed, I try to wipe my tears away, but they keep coming too fast.

"We're doing all right," Chris answers for both of us, putting his arm around me. When the volunteers momentarily leave, Chris leans over. "Our tickets have been changed. We don't have to fly out until Saturday or Sunday," he says. I feel the color drain from my face. In the chaos of everything else, I have not considered that we still need to go back to Colorado.

"Oh, no," I say, pulling away from his arms. "I'll take a train or we can rent a car, but I'm not flying. I'm done with planes, thank you very much."

Chris is about to say something, but our conversation is interrupted by the return of the Red Cross volunteer who apparently has caught the tail end of our conversation. "We have a room for each of you here. You don't have to decide tonight when you're leaving," she says sympathetically.

We thank her for her help and she introduces us each to our own personal concierge. A sweet little lady with a kind face extends her hand to me and introduces herself as Betty. I smile back at her. She immediately makes me feel at ease and I willingly follow her as she leads me to a table to pick out extra clothes. My clothes are presumably still in my suitcase sitting in the Hudson River. I pick out a pair of sweatpants and a tee shirt, a far cry from the carefully chosen outfits I had planned for our trip. Chris picks out a pair of jeans. We had each received sweatshirts from US Airways in the aftermath of the crash and we both put them on over our new clothes.

From there Betty leads me to another room full of tables where I will meet with a representative from the airlines. We are each assigned a US Airways representative who asks us a variety of questions about our flight before helping us get settled into our rooms. It is humbling to see how many strangers are willing to bend over backward to help us recover from our experience. I hope that I would do the same for others if given the chance. These strangers who have been thrust into my life have all demonstrated incredible sympathy and sensitivity and have helped to make a difficult situation much easier simply through their kindness.

Our friends Matt and Anna, who we had flown to New York to visit, have heard of our ordeal and they are on their way to the hotel to see us. We have just set foot in my hotel room when we hear a knock on the door. Matt and Anna come in with a rush of emotion and activity, shoving clothes into our arms before engulfing us in hugs.

"I brought you clothes," Anna says, and I am touched by her thoughtfulness. While I am thankful for the sweats and shirt I got from the Red Cross, I know that I will feel much better in clothes that actually fit me.

"How *are* you?" She asks in a tone that I will come to recognize over the next few months. It is a tone that implies that people know that you have experienced something life-changing.

"Good," I say and I honestly mean it. It is good to be dry and warm. It is good to be with Chris again and in the company of dear friends. Matt and Anna start a movie for us and Chris and I sink into the couch to relax. While we stare at the television, barely paying attention, our friends begin the arduous task of making phone calls to our family and friends to let them know that we are safe and sound. Without even asking, they know that we are already weary from answering so many questions about everything.

My room phone keeps ringing and to our surprise, one of the callers is a newsman from channel 9 news. "How did they find us?" I whisper to Chris as we put the call on speakerphone. They want to interview us and we happily oblige, telling our story one more time and hoping that it will be the last time for a long while.

The next day we are surprised to see paparazzi outside our hotel as we head out with Matt and Anna for breakfast. We are even more surprised when they start following us all over town.

"Can we ask you questions? Can we take pictures of you?" They ask. It flusters me. People who are celebrities may be used to this kind of attention, but I am no celebrity. The fact that my fifteen minutes of fame have arrived because of a traumatic event make it impossible for me to enjoy the attention.

It's an odd feeling to be newsworthy. If you are a part of a newsworthy experience but your experience is traumatic, you can't enjoy the fact that everyone wants to know about your story because you are somewhat disassociated with the reality of what happened to you. I was still processing what I had experienced and didn't have answers to the questions they were asking. It wasn't that I wanted to take interviews or anything, but it just seemed so weird to me that people would want to talk to me. I didn't know how to react. I can see now why, when people go through traumatic events and then get interviewed, they have no emotion.

For example, when a mother gives an interview after her child is abducted, people often say, "She has no emotion, so it's probably not real." In some cases it might not be real. But it also might be that she is still in shock. I can see why you might actually not have any emotion in response to a traumatic event. We were so in shock about the reality of what had happened to us that we hadn't made the connection yet and therefore, didn't have any emotions pouring out of us.

9

Going Home

Our plane went down on Thursday at 3:30 p.m. and after spending a few days recovering in New York we flew back to Colorado on Saturday morning (in spite of my earlier insistence that I would not fly). Chris's dad, a pilot, had flown out to be with us in New York and his presence was reassuring enough that I felt I could get on a plane again. I was thankful to be home and ready to move on with my life.

When we flew back into Denver, the airlines took special care of us, treating us like royalty on the flight. Landing in Denver is never smooth and it took all of my strength to not lose my cool during our descent. I was shaking as we disembarked, but overjoyed to see my family waiting for me directly outside the gate. The airport had bent the rules for us and allowed our family members special clearance in order to welcome us home. It was such a welcome sight to see them all standing there waiting for us; they even made signs. We were also met by news teams who keep yelling our names to get our attention. It felt odd not to have anything to pick up from baggage claim as we left the airport. All we had were the clothes on our backs.

We went to Chris's parents' house and told the story in full. With our family surrounding us and even more family members listening by phone, we relayed the details of our experience as well as we could, telling the story in bits and pieces. It felt good to be able to tell the people that we love most what we had been though. They listened intently, sometimes crying, sometimes thanking Jesus out loud for our safety. Our story ended and there were teary hugs all around. And then we ate cake.

After spending time reuniting with our families, I went home. It was Saturday night and I had to go to work the next day. My roommate greeted me with a hug but she didn't ask me much about my ordeal, and I was grateful for that. I was all talked out and I just wanted to fall into bed.

SECTION TWO

Celebrating

I will give thanks to you, Lord, with all my heart; I
will tell of all your wonderful deeds. I will be glad
and rejoice in you; I will sing the praises of your
name, O Most High.

Psalm 9:1–2

10

Statistics

Before we left for New York, I had arranged to be back at work the day after flying home. My job was one that I enjoyed, caring for an elderly woman. She was a high-needs patient and the job was quite physically demanding, a challenge that I enjoyed. My usual shift was thirty-six hours, Sunday through Tuesday morning. I was about to start my last semester at community college before my junior year at Metropolitan State University, and classes were to resume on Monday. I didn't think twice about going back to work because I didn't know any different.

I can't explain why I didn't take more time for myself before diving back into my pre-plane-crash life. Looking back, I know it wasn't the best choice, but I honestly felt that I was fine. I had worked through a lot of my issues with control in my early twenties and when the crash happened I naïvely assumed that I had already put in enough work to cover any backlash that might occur.

I could have at least taken a few days off work. (I mean, I had the mother of all excuses!) But that option didn't even cross my mind.

I just have to get back into it. I can't just stop my life to mull over what just happened, I told myself. I didn't want people to pity me or worry about me. I wanted to show them all that I was a survivor, both literally and emotionally. I was strong, strong enough to jump right back into life.

I told my patient's family what had happened and they were sympathetic. I told them that I was feeling tired, but fine.

"We'll give you time off," they told me.

"I really don't see the need for it," I reassured them. "I'm fine. I've got everything under control."

Working with my patient was a blessing. She slept through the night for the most part and I only had to get up with her a few times and then help her get ready in the morning. She enjoyed resting and being quiet. She liked to sit on her porch and listen to the birds. Honestly, working with her ensured that I took time to just rest as well. Yes, I had to take care of her and sometimes she could be difficult, but for the most part we just rested together, an imposed rest that I don't know that I would have sought out on my own. I am grateful to her for being my quiet companion. She didn't ask me questions about what I had been through and she didn't watch me for any signs of emotional distress. She just let me be. It was good for me to be with her because it created a space for calm in my life. If I hadn't been working I would have filled my time with mindless activities just to stay busy.

On Tuesday morning after I finished my first shift, I headed straight back to school. Life wasn't going to stop for me just because I could have died and I didn't know any other way except to keep going forward. I had a plan, after all, and I wanted to stick to it.

I was starting new classes and my first class of the day was a Statistics class. The professor was a woman I had known from a church I went to a long time ago. She knew of me because I had been friends with her daughter, but we weren't close. As soon as she handed out her syllabus, my heart dropped and I felt a wave of panic begin to wash over me. At the top of her syllabus, in bold, she had written the words, "How to Pass this Class and Avoid Landing in the Hudson."

I couldn't believe my eyes. I knew that we had made national news, but for some reason, I had expected to be able to forget about it while at school. It was a naïve thought.

"Oh my gosh," I gasped as I ran out of class. I started crying in the hallway as I desperately tried to reach Chris on my cell phone. When he answered I could barely explain, between my sobs, what had happened. I realized that I was having an irrational emotional response, but I couldn't explain it. It seemed ridiculous to me because I was sure that I was fine.

Every day I told myself that I was fine. I looked fine on the outside and I felt fine on the inside. So why was I crying so hard?

I had planned on telling my professors about the plane crash on the off chance that something like this might happen. I wasn't going to make a big deal about it; I was simply going to ask them to be patient with me because, despite the fact that I was going to try my best, I didn't know how I was going to perform in class. But I hadn't had a chance yet and here it was, smack-dab in my face.

Chris talked to me for several minutes until I felt calm enough to return to class, but I couldn't concentrate. My head was abuzz with emotion and I felt incapable of even hearing the lecture.

After class, I approached my teacher hesitantly.

"Hi," I said quietly, working up the courage to explain my abrupt exit earlier.

"Hi, Karin. Right?" She said, extending her hand to me.

"Yes. Um . . . I just want you to know that I was on the plane that crashed on the Hudson," I said, and as I watched my words sink in, a look of horror crossed her face.

"Oh, my goodness. I never would have thought . . . I am so sorry. I didn't know," she said, looking appalled.

"I'm not mad at you at all. You couldn't have known," I quickly reassured her. There was no way that she could have known, and the guilt on her face made me almost regret revealing my secret, but another part of me needed her to know.

I left, knowing that she felt awful, but also wondering about what had just happened. Statistically speaking, how likely was it for her to have written something about the plane crash and then to have a student who had been on the plane? She would probably be able to figure out the odds, being a statistics teacher and all, but it seemed improbable to me.

The next time I had class, my professor looked at me sympathetically and I knew that she still felt bad. I gave her an encouraging smile. I realized that I was going to have to be honest with the people in my life about what had happened to me. As much as I wanted to put it behind me and just move on, I also realized that my emotions could be triggered at any time and it wasn't fair to the people around me to have to deal with those emotions without knowing the root cause. It was a good lesson to learn.

After that, I told my teachers every semester, "I was in a plane crash. I am still processing. Sometimes I do well, sometimes I don't. I don't know what this semester is going to look like for me. I'm trying to move on, but I might have bad days." Every semester they responded with kindness and I began to feel better and better about telling people what I had been through.

11

Baggage

The desperate craving for control that I felt in my early twenties had lessened and I felt that I had worked through my issues for the most part. The plane crash was going to prove to be an opportunity for me to go deeper, like peeling an onion, but I didn't know it yet.

Following the crash, the aircraft, the pilots and everything else associated with the flight had to be investigated. This is standard practice and it takes a lot of time, but when an airplane crashes for whatever reason, people want to know why. When an airplane successfully lands on a body of water and there are no fatalities, people are especially interested in gaining a better understanding. As it turned out, the cause of our crash was a flock of geese flying beside our plane. It seemed a little crazy that a goose hitting our plane at the wrong spot could cause an entire plane to go down.

Since we had been a part of the crash, we had to answer questions as well as release our luggage to be weighed and examined thoroughly by the proper authorities. Although I understood why it was taking so much time, I was also a little annoyed to have to leave everything I had brought with me to New York with no promise as to when I might get it back.

At the end of February seven boxes in total arrived at my doorstep. Chris received boxes, too, at his address. Initially, I couldn't imagine what it could be, but then it occurred to me: Our luggage had finally made it back to Colorado more than a month after we had!

Everything we had taken with us had been separated into different bags and boxes. Everything was accounted for. My hair-ties had even been wrapped in tissue paper and numbered. Everything was itemized on a piece of paper and only one thing was missing—my big down coat from Eddie Bauer. I guess the Hudson River wanted to keep it along with the hat, scarf and necklace I had sacrificed to the ice.

Getting our stuff back was a little like Christmas. I had forgotten a few of the items that I had packed and it was fun and surprising to go through my belongings. They all had an industrialized scent, as though they had been washed in a heavy-duty detergent. I didn't enjoy the smell at all and immediately set about getting rid of it. Subconsciously, maybe I was trying to remove anything that might trigger memories of the crash. I got the smell out of most of my belongings, but couldn't quite remove it from one of my scarves. To this day every time I wear it, I smell the memories of our luggage, fished out of the Hudson River, inspected, categorized and sent home as an unexpected Christmas gift.

When we got back from New York, the National Transportation Safety Board (NTSB) called us and said there had never been a crash like this, where a plane landed in water and every passenger and even the plane survived. This news only added to my feelings of thankfulness. I was on an emotional high. I couldn't believe that we had been spared, and in such a miraculous way.

"That's amazing," I kept saying over and over again as they revealed new details from our crash. As time went on, we learn more about exactly what had happened.

The flight that we were on was supposed to take off at 3:05 p.m., but we didn't leave the gate until 3:20 p.m., fifteen minutes later. At the time, I remember thinking that I just wanted to get home and was a little put out by the delay.

We crashed at 3:31 p.m., which ended up being a crucial time for our rescue. The ferries on the Hudson River make their last trip at 3:30 p.m. and barges come from the north all the way down the river at that time as well. The ferries were ready and available to rescue us because they were preparing for their usual trip. If we had crashed at 3:15 p.m., who knows how long it would have taken for them to get to us? If we had crashed at 3:45 p.m., I cannot imagine how busy the traffic on the river would have been. We surely would have killed some unsuspecting people as we crashed into the river.

The north side of the Hudson was covered in ice that day, so the barges weren't able to come down the river as they usually did. The river was empty; no boats were on it, which made that landing possible. Yet there were ferries nearby, ready to rescue us in a timely manner.

It's amazing.

A few weeks before our trip to New York, I had started reading *Praying the Names of God*, by Ann Spangler. I had planned on reading a section the morning we left New York, but the morning had gotten away from me so I decided to read it during our flight. I never got the chance.

The study was about one of the names of God being *El Olam*—the everlasting and eternal God. One of the verses that this devotion referenced was Ecclesiastes 3:11 which says, "He has made everything beautiful in its time. He has also set eternity in the human heart; yet no one can fathom what God has done from beginning to end." It goes on to say that as Christians, we need to ask God to strengthen our hope in Him and our hope of heaven and that we need to give thanks for the promise of eternal life.

This book was in my luggage, tucked away in the bottom of the plane when we crashed. It went down with me into the river and just like me, it survived the ordeal. I got it back, water damage and all, when I received my luggage from the plane. When I realized this was the lesson for that day I got chills. I had intended to read it on the plane even though I forgot it in my luggage, but God intended for me to live it out. He knew that I liked to learn through experiences and He gave me a chance to do just that. Over the next two years, this question of "Who do I put my hope in?" would be put to the test. I would come to cling to the knowledge that my hope is in the promise of eternal life.

* * *

The true emotional impact of the crash didn't hit me until after we returned to Colorado and even then, it only hit me in small waves with days, sometimes weeks, between each wave. I thought that the incident in my statistics class was bad, but it didn't compare to what was soon to follow. I was completely unprepared for the emotional toll that the plane crash was going to take on me in the future. I was biding my time, unknowingly waiting for a wave so big it would take me months to recover.

In the meantime, I stayed busy.

It was good for me to get back into school and to feel as though my life had some sort of normalcy to it. I was not ready to process the emotional fallout of the crash, so I simply didn't. I didn't acknowledge my emotions and I didn't analyze how I was feeling. I simply lived, filling my days with work and school, so that I wouldn't have to take time to feel. People sometimes ask why I didn't take more time off and I tell them that I would have been wasting time, just sitting around and refusing to acknowledge my emotions.

12

Riding the Waves

Another "wave" occurred almost a month to the day after our crash. I had returned to work and to school with very little thought about the mental or emotional impact of my experience. Chris had almost seamlessly returned to his life, and I foolishly assumed that I could, too.

In February there was a plane crash in Buffalo, New York, and I was surprised by the violence of my response. Chris, my family, and even I (to a certain extent) expected both of us to not want to know anything about that crash. They assumed it would bring back too many memories. Just the opposite happened.

All of a sudden, I found that I couldn't get enough information about the crash. The cause of the Buffalo crash was ice buildup on the wing. All forty-nine passengers were killed as well as one person on the ground. As I glued myself to the news, I had a flash of realization that may seem dumb to some, but it was profound for me: I have been in a plane crash and I am alive. Intellectually, I realized how lucky we were to survive, but the Buffalo crash began a slowly unfolding emotional realization of how my life could have turned out differently.

* * *

My worries about my relationship with Chris had not dissipated, but I felt more patient about my relationship with him.

Much of this is due to the fact that I daily reminded myself of what God told me while we were waiting to be rescued. "I do not need to worry about when Chris is going to propose," I told myself. What's more, I believed it. "This is apparently not the right time and I'm OK with that."

Following our return to Colorado, I realized that we were both in a fragile state and that we both needed to figure out what we needed in life outside of one another. It was not the time to be nagging him about the question of "us." I grudgingly accepted the fact that I had been rather annoying with my questions about where our relationship was headed. Before the crash, I had been desperate to know what he wanted from me and what our future was going to look like and I had communicated those questions to him. Several times.

I didn't have the energy to bother with those questions anymore. God had other things for me to focus on, like figuring out how to make it through each day. I lived in a constant state of readiness and paranoia because I didn't know when emotions were going to impede my ability to function in my day-to-day world. Some days I felt fine. Other days, I struggled.

In March, two months after the crash, Chris took me on a special date.

"I've never been more confident than I am today that you are the woman that I want to be with," Chris said, unprompted, after we had ordered our food. His words warmed my heart and I smiled at him. But I knew not to press him further.

OK. That doesn't mean he's going to propose soon, it just means he's confident, I reminded myself. It signaled progress in our relationship, because for so long when he had said he loved me and cared about me he almost always seemed to follow it up with, "I'm just not sure that I'm ready to dive in."

Before our trip to New York we had been at a crossroads. After dating for three years, I knew that we were both thinking that same thing: *Should we stay together or is it time to go our separate ways?*

Our relationship had been on the rocks, and yet we knew that we had to make it through the end of January because we were going on that trip together. It seems like a horrible reason to stay together, just because you had bought plane tickets, but God knew what He was doing. He had bigger things in store for us on that trip besides spending some time with friends.

God, I can't do this, I had prayed over and over again during the several months that Chris and I dated long-distance due to his job (he had spent three months in Germany). *He's been so far away. He says he loves me, but doesn't seem to want to marry me. How much longer does he need before he can commit? I just need to know. Show Chris what he needs to see to make a decision about me. Do something in his life to make him see whether he wants me in his life or not.*

Chris was standing next to me on the wing of the plane with water quickly rising when he felt God speak to him: *Karin is amazing and you don't know how long you have.*

The reality of what had just happened came crashing down on him and he, in a second, realized that tomorrow is never promised. Unbeknownst to me, God was softening Chris's heart in the very way that I had asked for. It was so far from the way I would have hoped for it to happen.

"You know, Karin, I realized that I'll never have all my ducks in a row. I needed to learn that I don't have to have it all together to marry you," Chris told me that night in March after the crash. My heart sped up and I felt my face getting hot. I didn't expect him to propose on the spot, but to hear him say something I had so longed to hear brought great hope and peace for our future together.

I realized that I needed to sit back and let God work. In other words, I needed to relinquish control. It wasn't my job to make things move forward, and by trying to push them forward, I had actually caused myself more pain and exasperation. Never in a million years would I have asked for a plane crash to make Chris realize he wanted to marry me, but "in all things God works for the good of those who love him, who have been called according to his purpose" (Romans 8:28).

13

A Proposal

During the years I spent waiting for Chris, I learned that we will come to many crossroads in our lives, both individually and as a couple, and how we proceed is imperative to the outcome. After the crash, we had to realize that we had a shared goal which was to be together forever, but how we got there was so different. We had to struggle with how to honor each other in that process without stepping on each other's toes. I realized that my way of dealing with difficult decisions and situations works for me, but it doesn't work for everyone and it doesn't always work for Chris.

I resolved to be patient and to allow Chris to handle our relationship the way he thought best. It was difficult for me to let go and trust, but I knew that if I wanted this relationship to last, I needed to practice relinquishing control.

The day I had been longing for happened in June on the cliffs of Rhode Island.

We were there as honored guests for a celebratory weekend for Lockheed Martin employees. While I was terrified to fly again, I was thrilled at the prospect of traveling with Chris. Before we left, I prayed that this trip would be less trauma-filled than the last.

During some of our free time we decided to explore Rhode Island. We brought a camera with us as we walked along the cliffs and even though I had been using the camera all day, Chris had been weirdly protective of the case, not letting me hold it at all.

As we walked along the cliffs we stopped periodically to take pictures and simply take in the view. The views were breathtaking and I couldn't help but close my eyes and breathe deeply the smell of the sea.

"Let's go down here," he says, pointing to a walkway.

We walk slowly down to the edge of the water and dip our toes into the chilly waters. We sit together quietly, each consumed with our own thoughts. I take that chance to talk to God.

You know what, God? I'm so glad that Chris and I have this time together. Thank you for allowing us to come on this trip. I really am so thankful that Chris and I are together. I realize that for the first time in a long while, I am content to just be.

Suddenly, Chris stands up, breaking into my prayers. I assume he is uncomfortable sitting on the rocks and so I don't look up until he speaks.

"C'mon, you ready to go?" he asks, giving me his hand.

"Sure," I respond. I stand up and Chris surprises me by wrapping his arms around me. He doesn't seem ready to go at all and I look at him quizzically.

"I just want you to know how much I really love you," he says, staring at me intently.

"I love you too. Isn't this so much fun? What a great trip," I say, still thinking we are heading out.

"I just want you to know that I want to be able to do these things with you forever." As he gets down on one knee, the realization of what is happening hits me.

"You're kidding me! No way! You're kidding," I say, and I hear myself laughing.

"Karin, will you marry me?" He asks, once I have calmed down enough to stop talking.

"Of course I'll marry you," I say. There has never been any doubt in my mind about whether or not I want to marry him.

He slips a gorgeous ring onto my finger and stands to kiss me.

There on the cliffs of Rhode Island, the thing that I have prayed for and dreamed about finally comes true. I know that I am blessed. I have cheated death and now I am going to get to marry the man of my dreams. For the rest of our time in Rhode Island I feel like I am walking on air.

* * *

We hit horrendous turbulence flying back into Colorado just as we had when we flew home from New York, only this time we were on a much smaller plane. Before our plane took off, I had introduced myself to the passenger sitting next to me, a sweet little lady from Colorado. Now, as our plane bounced up and down, I squeezed her hand until I heard her yelp in pain. Chris could see the panic in my eyes and he tried to calm me, but I was barely holding on. There was only one thing that kept me calm. I reminded myself, *I am engaged!* and *There is no way that I am going to die before getting married.*

14

A Wedding

The next few months went by like a whirlwind as I prepared for our wedding and my move to Colorado Springs to be with Chris. I knew where I wanted to get married even before Chris proposed: the Ryssby Chapel in Longmont, Colorado. My big sister, Sarah, had gotten married there and her wedding had been beautiful. Since Sarah and I have always had a close relationship, I loved the idea of getting married in the same location, and she did, too.

In October I decided to quit my job. I had been feeling run down, and my neck, which I had injured slightly in the crash, had been giving me problems. The neck muscles spasmed periodically, causing severe pain and headaches that left me weary and disoriented. I couldn't sleep well when the muscles spasmed. I also couldn't work out, something that was driving me crazy. My neck problem had been making my job more difficult, especially the lifting. And knowing that I would have to quit eventually in order to move to Colorado Springs, I decided to take an early leave. I had saved up some money to live on until my wedding in December and I was excited to devote my time to planning my future nuptials. Quitting my job signaled the end of a chapter in my life and it seemed fitting that I begin the next chapter of my life as a married woman in a new city with a new job.

It was a nice luxury not to work for a couple of months. I threw myself into planning our wedding and making the most of the time I had left in Boulder. I met with friends between running here and there, finalizing the details for our big day. I felt as though I was on an emotional high from getting engaged and I didn't want it to end, so I didn't allow myself a lot of down time. I kept myself busy, skipping from one task to the next. *I am finally getting married!* After waiting years for engagement to happen, I was determined to make the most of my experience.

* * *

Chris and I got married on December 31, 2009, in a winter wedding ceremony. You often hear of all the things that go wrong at weddings, but I don't feel like anything went wrong for ours. Perhaps something did, but almost losing our lives in a plane crash definitely helped me keep things in perspective. Our wedding took place in a beautiful candlelight service at the chapel. A fantastic reception, complete with dessert and appetizers, followed. We danced and mingled and even received a special message from Captain "Sully," the hero pilot of Flight 1549.

Getting married and moving to Colorado Springs signaled a fresh start in life for me. Even though my life had been wonderful before, I was eager to begin again. Life was simple in Colorado Springs and the pace that I had become used to pre-wedding settled down significantly. I signed up for classes and only worked a few hours a week in order to focus on my studies. I spent my time setting up our home and being a new wife. I didn't have any friends because I was new to town and all of my old friends lived a two-hour car ride away. Surprisingly, I was OK with this. I had Chris and I didn't feel lonely at all.

So life was quiet, which was good, but that led to something that I was unprepared for. The longer I lived in Colorado

Springs, the more my pace of life slowed down. The more the pace of life slowed down, the lonelier I got. I began to feel isolated, away from my friends. Yet, I didn't feel that I had the energy to meet new ones. As I struggled with my feelings of loneliness and isolation, the crash resurfaced.

SECTION THREE

Sinking

An abnormal reaction to an abnormal situation is normal behavior.

Viktor E. Frankl[3]

15

Return to New York

In January of 2010 we flew back to New York for the one-year anniversary of the plane crash. We had been married only a week. On the flight into New York, I felt even more nervous than on the flight out of New York the year before. A year ago on our way into the city I had been so excited about seeing the famous New York landmarks and I been so consumed with excitement and hope. This time, I didn't want to look out the window at all. I just kept my eyes closed and prayed the entire time.

"Know what?" Chris asks as soon as we land.

"Don't tell me we did the flight pattern backwards," I say, peering at him through one opened eye, my hands still gripping to armrests.

"Yep," he says squeezing my hand. I can't read the expression on his face, but I feel sure that everyone can read the expression on mine.

The reunion was a joyful time despite the stress of the flight. We got to reconnect with other passengers from Flight 1549 and share how our lives had changed since the crash. It was an interesting reunion because even though we had been through a shared experience, we had gone through it as strangers. Coming back together, we already knew one of the most significant events of each other's lives, and yet we didn't really know the simplest details that you usually find out when you get to know people. It was almost as if the process of meeting these people had been reversed.

Flying *out* of New York after the one-year anniversary celebration was horrible. It took everything in me to not break down in a full panic attack. As the flight took off, I felt as if I were reliving the crash. I started counting the seconds; replaying everything in my mind about the day we crashed.

This was when we hit the birds, was one of my first thoughts. This was quickly followed by, *Thank God we made it past that point. Thank God we're still in the air.*

When the seatbelt sign went off, I felt a little better, but not much. When I saw the flight attendants walking back and forth, I finally began to relax because I knew that we were safe. We were past the point where we crashed.

I was adamant that the crash would be *an* event in my life, not *the* event of my life. I realized that it was life-changing. However, I was not willing to be defined by one event, albeit a traumatic one. *How do I incorporate this event into my life without letting it take over?* became a daily question that I asked myself. *How do I weave it into who I am and what I am doing so that it inspires me instead of hindering me?* I didn't have the answers at that point.

I had done a decent job of not letting it define me during the first year after the crash. I simply refused to give it any space in my life. I moved through my day-to-day activities with a positive outlook. I dove back into my life and kept myself so busy that I didn't have time to process what happened emotionally.

I had to keep it all together. I had already paid for school and my books. I needed to work to support myself. The crash happened five days before class started. I was not going to just drop out of school. I didn't think I had any option except to go ahead with my life. There were times where I knew that I hadn't dealt with the emotional side effects of the crash, but I did not know how to make the time or space in my life to do so. Also, I didn't really want to.

There are no manuals about how to process surviving a plane crash, no Twelve-Step programs to wellness. I just did the best I could.

Before the crash I had felt a sense of accomplishment and purpose because I had taken a few years off school and then had finally made up my mind to go back and get my degree. I had originally thought that I wanted to be a nurse, but when I realized that nursing wasn't my calling I found a program for social work and I was excited about it. I didn't want to give up my goals. I found comfort in diving back into my life and doing what I needed to do. I don't think I recognized that it was just a way to numb my emotions. I couldn't handle the reality of what had happened. I was running away from it.

After the crash, I started hearing news updates about planes crashing around the world. I didn't know if the number of planes crashing had gone up or if I had been made more aware of them through my own experience. Anytime I heard of a plane crash, I felt panicky and sick. At first, I thought it might be therapeutic for me to learn about each incident in as much detail as possible because it would make me appreciate my survival more, but as time went on Chris mentioned that it didn't seem to help me at all. It only hurt me and made me more emotional. He was right, but a habit had been formed: Whenever I learned of a plane crash, I binged on information until I had worked myself into an emotional frenzy. Each scenario just made me feel worse and they raised a lot of questions for me.

I wondered, *Why did God choose to spare every single person on our flight, but He allows others to die?*

That made me wonder, *Does my life have more meaning than others? Does what I do really matter?* I was asking questions that usually come with a midlife crisis—and I was in my twenties.

I'd always taken jobs that require caring for other people such as being a Certified Nurse's Assistant or a nanny. I care about people. I have outward focus. I like helping people, but even with jobs that are built around serving others I was still asking, *Does what I am doing matter? At the end of the day, if I wasn't here, would I be missed?*

Thus I began an unhealthy obsession with the hurt, pain and deaths that were occurring all around me in the world, starting with those people who had lost their lives in the Buffalo crash and extending to any news event I happened to hear about. I didn't have mere curiosity like people who drive by a car crash and crane their necks to get a glimpse; I had an unhealthy, all-consuming obsession.

When we landed safely in Colorado I believed that I could put it all behind me instead of dealing with it. It had worked to suppress my emotions for a while, but apparently when people experience something as traumatic as narrowly avoiding untimely death, it is only a matter of time before they are forced to deal with it.

I began to believe a lie: that no one had ever been through what I had been through and therefore, no one would understand. For me, the crash that had once felt so miraculous began to feel isolating, even though Chris had been with me. We were on totally different roads with it. Because I bought into this isolating lie, I was reluctant to reach out for the help I needed when my emotions began to feel out of control. I really didn't think anyone could truly understand.

16

And So It Begins . . .

A documentary was made about our flight. When I told Chris about it, he made it clear that he would not be watching it. "I lived it," he says. "I don't need to watch a documentary."

I wished that I felt the same, but my obsession with death had taken root and I knew that I had to watch it. And so I did. I watched every second of it, barely taking time to blink.

It was a huge mistake. Before the documentary was even over I started crying, and I would not stop for what felt like the next six months.

"That was us, that was really us," I kept repeating even as my eyes were glued to the television. On the day of the crash while we were watching the news footage of the crash and we were seeing ourselves standing on the wing of the plane, we knew that we were seeing ourselves, but the event was still so fresh that it didn't make an emotional impact. I was able to say, "I was on that plane" immediately after the crash. But saying, "I was on the plane" and understanding what that meant for me emotionally took a whole year for me to come to terms with.

It was real to me mentally because I couldn't deny all of the proof that I had been a part of the crash, but emotionally I had been in denial. For so long, I had detached myself from reality because it was too traumatic, but when I watched that documentary, all my previous defenses proved useless and reality came crashing down on me. I was totally unprepared.

By the end of March, I felt as if all of my fears and the emotions that I had suppressed were fighting their way to the surface, determined to make me acknowledge them. I was choking on emotions. I started to feel that I was sinking under the sheer intensity of what I was feeling. Every day I seemed to fall deeper and deeper into this dark emotional state and I didn't know how to adequately express how I was feeling, let alone how to make it stop. My emotions were consuming me, and I literally felt as if I were drowning.

I started to process what had happened. Instead of just brushing off my feelings or trying to paint an optimistic picture, I began to constantly relive the moments immediately following the crash. As time went on, my fears and anxieties became worse and worse and every day I felt as if it took every ounce of my strength to just wake up.

* * *

One day all my anxieties and worries come to a head. It started early in the night.

We were driving home from my parents' house about an hour away and I just happened to look over at Chris in the driver's seat. When I couldn't see his seatbelt, my anxiety began to rise.

"Chris, are you wearing your seatbelt?" I asked.

"Yeah," he said, pulling it up with his thumb as proof.

"Good," I said, sitting back in my seat, but I didn't feel relaxed. I could feel him looking at me from across the car, but I didn't make eye contact.

I started to wonder why I had asked him about his seatbelt. My mind began to race. The day of the crash, I had asked Chris how planes fly and then we crashed. A small part of me felt as though I had jinxed us. I knew that I didn't have that kind of power, but it still bothered me. If I had asked how planes fly and then we crashed, did that mean I had a premonition? Was I having a premonition now? Were we going to get into a car accident? Why did I ask him about his seatbelt?

The whole way home I was tense, waiting for something to happen. I wondered if God had given me an insight into what was going to happen. I wondered if He would do that, and if so, why?

It was a windy night and the stress of worrying the whole ride home had gotten to me. My day had been horrible because I had been on the move and I hadn't eaten much except for coffee and some desserts; the ride home just made me feel more upset. Chris told me that he was going to bed. But try as I might, I couldn't calm down enough to sleep. I sat in bed, trying to relax, but to no avail. The wind outside kept me awake and even though Chris was sleeping peacefully beside me, I couldn't calm myself down. All of my fears and anxieties, coupled with the sweets and caffeine, combined into the perfect storm. I was exhausted, not just from the day, but from the load that I had been carrying since the crash. I was sick of feeling emotional. Even though I knew that I was not thinking clearly, I couldn't shake the feeling that something bad was going to happen. Was it the start of a catastrophic event? An earthquake? My mind even began thinking it could be the Rapture.

I know what you're thinking: *Whoa. The Rapture? Isn't that a bit extreme?*

Yes, it was extreme. I knew that my train of thought was crazy, but I couldn't stop it which just made me feel even crazier.

I convinced myself that the wind was a signal and as I sat and waited for whatever was in store, I couldn't do anything but cry and pray. The harder the wind blew, the more my anxiety grew.

An argument that Chris and I had had played through my mind: "Why are you so afraid? Just stop your emotions and you won't feel anxious anymore," he had said to me when I had approached him about my fears. He wasn't trying to be mean or insensitive; that is just the way Chris is. He is logical and he really did not understand that I couldn't just stop feeling the way that I was feeling.

"It just isn't working. I can't stop it!" I had yelled, feeling frustrated with him and me. "I know this is stupid and doesn't make sense. It doesn't make sense, but I can't stop my emotions."

God, I just don't want to feel like this. Why am I feeling like this? I don't want to feel like this anymore. I am not going to live like this. I'm not going to live my life thinking that a panic attack is right around the corner. Why am I letting myself get to this point? I asked Him this over and over again as I sat and waited. I recognized that the crash had not only affected me more than I let on, but that the effects of the crash had started controlling my life. I no longer had control over my emotions and I knew that to go on living in my current state would be no life at all. I was more exhausted than I had ever been before physically, mentally, emotionally and spiritually.

I didn't know what to do. I felt my panic rising to a point that I had never experienced in my entire life. I didn't know what to do. I felt like I was going to die. I didn't want to disturb Chris because I already felt like such a burden to him (a feeling that weighed on me more than I let on). I also felt like a failure as a wife. Chris thought he was marrying a perky, optimistic, fun woman and he ended up with me. Besides, Chris has been through the exact same thing, but he didn't seem to having a hard time with it at all. What was *wrong* with me?

At 1:00 a.m. I called my sister, Sarah, from the floor of our living room.

"Where's Chris?" she asked after I choked out a brief explanation.

"He's sleeping. He just doesn't understand," I sobbed into the phone.

"Karin, Chris loves you and I love you and God loves you, too. Talk to Chris. Let him know how you are feeling. You can't do this on your own."

"I can't," I continued to weep. "He just doesn't get it."

"Can I pray for you?" Sarah asked, and for the first time that night I felt a little bit of hope.

"Yes," I whispered.

"God, Karin needs you right now. She needs to know that you love her and that you are in control and that you are concerned for her. Let her feel your love and your healing presence at this moment, please. Give her peace. Amen."

It was a simple prayer, but it was exactly what I needed to hear. I needed to be reminded that God loves me. I needed His peace that passes all understanding, because trying to chase peace on my own was not working. Although God had allowed me to experience such a difficult moment in my life, God was still concerned for me. This was the thought that was most eye-opening to me as I hung up the phone with my sister.

There in my home, at 1:00 a.m., with the wind howling outside our windows, I finally surrendered control. I gave all of my fears and my anxieties to Jesus.

17

Logic

The next morning I woke up still feeling anxious, but I also had made up my mind: I am not going to live in a state of constant anxiety anymore. I am not going to believe that panic attacks are constantly right around the corner. It was a defining moment for me because I had finally allowed myself to be honest with Sarah about my emotional state. I found it freeing to reveal my innermost fears and to be loved in spite of them. It gave me the confidence I needed to seek help.

I realized that I may always have panic attacks, but that I don't have to live my life waiting for them. I can do things to prevent them. I don't have to live like a powerless victim in my own life. I have power. And more importantly, I have God backing me up, waiting for me to ask for His help. I identified my unhealthiness and called it by name and made up my mind to try and take some control back in my own life.

It would not be an easy fix. I honestly did not even know where to start, but I did feel that I must share honestly with Chris how I had been feeling. I knew that I would still struggle with anxiety, but that Chris would eagerly partner with me in the healing process.

Chris is logical. There will be many times when I start falling apart emotionally and I know it, but I can't seem to pull myself out of the pit I am in. Chris can recognize that and can simply talk to me calmly and rationally. He can offset my emotionality with his rational thinking. And sometimes getting rational is the only way for me to feel any semblance of peace.

I went through a time in which my thoughts seemed so illogical that I thought I might actually be going crazy. Chris offered a grounding presence in my life, especially during my darkest times. He helped to calm me down.

I began to understand that the very thing that frustrated me about Chris on the night of my breakdown is the thing that will help me in the long run. Chris is logical and I am emotional. We are different, but we work well together. It isn't Chris's fault that he didn't understand what I was going through. He processed the crash in a different way than I did. I couldn't get mad at him for that. His suggestion probably would have worked for him and he was just trying to help because he loved me.

I also started to realize that in the name of helping, people will often step on your toes. They will say things and do things that may seem unkind and less than helpful, but they usually mean well. They're just trying to help within the limitations of their own knowledge and their understanding and they are suggesting what they believe to be beneficial. It may work. Or it might not. What works for one person doesn't necessarily work for all.

I learned that I would have to communicate what I need and what I want. I would have to say, "I don't need *this*, but I need you to do *that* instead. I need you to ask me how I'm doing because I'm not doing well. I just want you to listen." I would just have to speak up about what I needed and I would have to be clear because otherwise I might inadvertently get hurt more. People will try to do what they think is in your best interest, but they cannot always be right. They may be overwhelmed by their desire to help. They may want to be there for you, but they don't know how to. It's not their fault that they don't.

I began to learn a lot about myself. I got more in tune with who I am and how I feel and what's going on around me. I had always been good at perceiving what other people are thinking and feeling, but now I needed to do that for myself, which can be uncomfortable at times. I had always been able to tell when I was emotionally not doing well and I could usually identify why—in the past. But lately, I found it impossible. I no longer knew why I felt the way I did. I didn't know why I would start to think certain thoughts or feel certain emotions. I could not tell you *why;* I only knew one thing: *I just am this way.* It can be enormously frustrating to feel out of control when it comes to one's own thoughts and emotions.

I had shifted into a new role that I had never experienced before and it scared me. I felt lost, out of control and honestly, potentially crazy. My emotions were the problem; I was not acting out or being unsafe. I was not delusional, and I was not experiencing a psychological breakdown. I was just feeling "crazy" because I couldn't believe the thoughts I was having about dying and death.

I couldn't tell you why I was afraid of dying, but I was. The surface reason for this was obvious: I had been in a plane crash. But my fear was getting way out of control and it seemed to go much deeper than simply knowing I cheated death. I felt death all around me and there didn't seem to be an escape.

I became obsessed with death, dying and how I would eventually die. Without even trying, my mind would wander to thoughts of how I might die and I would play through what I would do if each of them happened to me. This was just another extension of my need to plan. I thought that if

I could mentally go through every death scenario and think about how I would respond, I would somehow keep the worst from occurring. And then if it did, at least I would be prepared because I had already imagined it.

18

Unpacking My Emotions

Despite my resolve to get better, I was constantly living in a state of fear. This time I couldn't just will myself to do something. I hated it and realized that I couldn't live this way forever, but something in me told me that I would never recover if I didn't feel the entirety of my emotions. Instead of stuffing them away, I needed to air them out in order to start to heal.

So that's what I did. Unpacking my response to the crash was like unpacking a suitcase, but because I had jammed everything in there for so long, my emotions were flinging themselves out of the suitcase violently instead of coming out in an organized and orderly manner. It was not pretty, to say the least. At last I understood that I needed to accept myself just as I was and not try to hide it or fix it.

When I felt as if decisions had been made for me, I struggled; it's part of that whole control issue that I couldn't quite seem to conquer. In the past if I wanted something, I went out to get it. I was a doer; I worked hard in order to pay for my own college education. The realization that I didn't know how to control my emotions was upsetting to me.

My need to plan everything in advance seemed to be amplified after the crash. I wanted to be in control even more. I wanted to control everything, big and small, because it seemed to be the only thing that gave me a sense of peace. I wanted to know, When am I going to see you again? Do we have money in savings? What are our plans for the future?

Knowing more about everything and talking more about how I was feeling helped me to plan ahead. It also helped me to predict possible emotional landmines. I could say, "OK, I know that life is going to be hard, but I am planning this really fun thing in the future" and that helped me. I was aware that my need for control was unhealthy, but that was the way it was and I would have to be OK with that. I knew that God had said to not worry (in Matthew 6:34) and that He has a plan (in Jeremiah 29:11), but I continued to struggle with what it really looks like to surrender to God. What did it look like to fully surrender to Him, to know that He is in control and to fully trust him? I wanted that. Desperately.

I was trying, but there were still parts of me that I couldn't seem to relinquish. It felt too scary to give everything over to Him. God was gracious with me, though. I didn't think God was mad at me over this issue of control. I didn't think He was looking at His watch, saying, "You should be over this by now. Get over it. I'm in control." Rather, though He was saying, "I know what that feels like. I know how scary that is for you."

Something that helped me come to terms with everything was the parable of the ten virgins found in Matthew 25. Referring to Christ's return, it speaks of preparedness in a positive light. At the end of the chapter we are charged with keeping watch, "because you do not know the day or the hour" (Matthew 25:13). This helped me to see that God speaks of preparedness in positive terms and that planning is not a bad thing. I just needed to be mindful about putting my human plans above God's perfect ones.

19

My Relationship with God

I haven't always felt close to God. I had been going to church since I was a child and I had always had faith. But like most people, I also went through a time of doubt. Mine occurred in high school. I had resentment toward God because my parents decided to pull me out of public school and homeschool me through high school. I didn't want to be homeschooled because I felt that I would miss out on crucial life experiences. I also didn't want to be away from my friends.

I was mad at God because I felt that He told my parents to take me out of school. "Why did you do that?" I would ask Him over and over again. "It doesn't make sense!"

I was bitter because I felt like He was unfair. It took me a while to realize that it was for the best.

In college, I was able to see the blessing. I had been protected from my friends who were making choices that did not align with my principles. I liked my friends, but they were making life choices that I couldn't support and looking back, I don't know if I could have withstood the peer pressure.

The summer after my freshman year, I finally repented and surrendered all of my bitterness and frustration to Jesus. "I'm not mad at You. I trust You. I need Your forgiveness for being so angry and bitter for so long," I told Him, even though He already knew my heart.

In spite of this, my faith was still on shaky ground. I had a lot of questions, the biggest being whether or not I actually mattered to God. I knew that God loved me in a general humanity kind of way, but I wondered, *Does he actually care for me, Karin?* After the plane crash, all of these questions, which had lain dormant for some time, came rushing back.

I guess sometimes it is easier to just say that I know that God loves us and He saved us and He forgives us. However, believing that God actually cares about what I am feeling and struggling with? That's harder. I was having a hard time trusting that He was not just expecting me to fix my own brokenness and get better and be more available for His Kingdom. God doesn't have that kind of an agenda. But sometimes, I was putting an agenda on myself: I should be reading my Bible every day and I should be praying. I should be growing. I felt guilty that I was struggling, as if my faith wasn't strong enough to deal with my situation. Then I realized that God calls us all to different things and this is what He had called me to for now.

I think God knows how scared I was about all of this, and therefore He was being tender toward me. Before He had Moses bring the people out of their bondage, God shares that He was concerned about the suffering of the Israelites in Egypt:

> The Lord said, "I have indeed seen the misery of my people in Egypt. I have heard them crying out because of their slave drivers, and I am concerned about their suffering. (Exodus 3:7)

This verse was and continues to be so comforting to me. To think that God not only knows when I am suffering, but that he is also *concerned* that I am suffering!

It was too easy for me to slip into this mindset of thinking, *God is mad at me because I'm not better and I'm not obeying him well enough*. But I don't think that's how He works. Really that was me projecting my insecurities onto Him, which is not right. His kindness is what leads us through hard times; I needed to remember that. Instead of being mad at me because I'm not completely surrendering or because I am struggling; I think He's sad that I'm hurting.

There was a point in my life where I couldn't get enough of time with God. I did a daily devotion and spent hours on my knees talking to Jesus about every aspect in my life. Those times were long gone. I just didn't have the emotional energy for it anymore. It sounds like a lame excuse, but working through emotions is draining. Sometimes I wished that I was back there, able to pray constantly and feeling like God was guiding my every step. I really wanted to be back there. But that was not where I was at. It didn't mean that my faith was any less or more; it was just the way it was.

Since this was where God was allowing me to be, I would just have to honor and bless it. If I ran away from it, I would miss an opportunity to grow.

Even realizing this, still I was wrestling with the belief that God honestly cares about the fears and emotions of Karin Rooney. Then I read about the Israelites in the book of Exodus. They were in slavery and they called out to God: "God heard their groaning and he remembered his covenant with Abraham, with Isaac and with Jacob. So God looked on the Israelites and was concerned about them" (Exodus 2:24–25). This verse offered me the hope that God could be concerned about me specifically—Karin—not just humankind in general.

20

Uncertainty

There was a time when I didn't want to read the Bible and I didn't want to pray because I thought that if I got close to God that He was going to ask me to give up my life. I felt that if I really entrusted my life to God, if I really said, "Your will be done" and actively lived like that, it would ultimately mean my death. That scared me. I loved God, but I wasn't ready to sacrifice my life for Him. Which of course made me feel guilty.

What I had to remember is that just following God doesn't mean that He is going to ask me to sacrifice my life in His name. Yes, He has asked that of some, but not of all of His followers. And if He ever did ask it, He would walk us through that time. God cares about us and He isn't just out there to have us die for His glory and His name.

However, for a while I wondered if that was a part of His plan.

I wouldn't say that I'm radical, but I believe that if you pray for it, God will do it. I believe in praying big prayers and aligning my heart with God and His Word so that my prayers are in line with His. After all, He had answered my prayers about Chris in a huge way. I used to be able to pray like that but I stepped back from it a bit during the aftermath of the crash.

I was wrestling with what it meant for me and how it would translate into my life. Before, it was easy to say, "I'm going to live for God. I'm going to do whatever he wants me to do." After the crash, I was more aware of the cost.

When you really think about it, none of us can know what He may have in store for us. That's scary, especially for a planner like me.

Denise, my longtime mentor and friend, once told me that when you're young, it's easy to be on a faith roller coaster. You go to the Christian camp and you come back high on the Lord and then in real life you make mistakes and you're really hard on yourself. And then you repeat the cycle over and over again, as much as your parents will allow.

As you get older, your life starts to even out, but it still maintains elements of a roller coaster, although your ups and downs may be more extreme. You might have a really crazy up and a really crazy down, but you're not going to be so continuously up and down as when you were a teen. You're learning what that looks like to just be more stable as a person and a Christian, not driven by emotions, but truth.

Before the crash, I felt that if I could only get Chris to propose and we could just get married, life would be stable for me. I thought that if I achieved that goal, my life would be ideal. Now I realize that life is anything but stable. It is full of trauma and adventure and you never know what is just around the corner.

At the Katie Couric Show with Elaina in 2013. I and other passengers were asked to come and share how our lives had changed since the crash. Photo Credit: Karin Rooney

A CURE FOR COLD FEET
Chris Rooney & Karin Hill (seats 18D, 18E)

Karin Hill and Chris Rooney had been dating for three years when they boarded Flight 1549. "We were getting to the point when we had to decide if we would get married or call it off," says Chris, 24. "I had been indecisive. I felt I had to be certain that I could dedicate myself to Karin." Hill had no doubts, but "I didn't want him to marry me then later say he did it only because I wanted it." But after the crash, "I started seeing Karin in a new light," says Chris, an engineer. "I wanted to protect her always." When he proposed in June, "I had no idea it was coming," says Karin, 25, who is studying to be a social worker. Their

New Year's Eve wedding in Boulder, Colo., featured a taped toast from hero pilot Capt. Chesley Sullenberger. Says Chris: "We could not be more excited to start our lives together.".

The groom's cake.

The wedding day.

We were featured in *People* Magazine one year after the crash along with other passengers who had experienced big life changes after the crash. We had married **December 31, 2009**. Photo Credit: *People* Magazine and William J. Meyer Photography

Karin, Elaina and Sully backstage at the Katie Couric show. Photo Credit: Karin Rooney

Tripp Harris was in the raft near the front of the plane. He captured three photos of passengers on the wing. Chris and I were standing against the fuselage. Photo Credit: Tripp Harris

Rooney family, 2016. Photo Credit: Karin Rooney

Rex Babin drew this illustration after the crash and it was featured in the *Sacramento Bee*. As the plane was crashing, the Lord had given me the words, "lay this plane down gently." This illustration was my prayer; I was amazed that someone else saw the power of God that day and was led to offer this for the world to see.

Photo credit: Tripp Harris

April 2017 after our son, Henry, was born. Photo Credit: Erin Lenzini Photography

21

A Woman with a Plan

I couldn't seem to stop my compulsive planning. Even after wrestling with and finally reaching a place where I was OK with it (although I don't think anybody else was), I couldn't seem to stop. I felt that I needed to plan everything down to the smallest detail to keep my anxiety at bay, so I kept planning.

I don't like being irrational, but at the same time, I couldn't seem to stop it. I was self-aware enough to know when I was thinking irrational things, but unfortunately not self-aware enough to know how to handle it well. Or how to change it.

I felt that people were judging me and questioning my relationship with God because I struggled so much. Maybe some people were, but I know that for the most part, I was just assuming they thought that way because I was questioning my relationship with God. I worried too much about how others might perceive me. Of course it doesn't matter what other people think. I don't have to explain myself. And if people don't like or understand my behavior, well, I don't need them in my life, at least for that season. I needed to surround myself with people who were OK with the process that I was in, who could support me and encourage me. I did not need the people who just wanted me to be better because my struggle made them uncomfortable.

* * *

I realized just how much I needed to plan one weekend when I was talking to my sister on the phone. Sarah and her husband were going to come to Colorado Springs from Boulder for the weekend, and I keep insisting that we nail down an exact time and day.

"Are you coming down Friday night or Saturday night? Because we're having dinner with friends on Friday night. So if you want to come down you can, but you might be by yourselves until seven or eight because we won't be home until later," I told her, not for the first time. I could hear myself repeating the same things over and over again, but something in me felt panicked about not knowing exactly when they would arrive.

"Why are you so worried about it? Why are you freaking out? We're coming down this weekend. You don't have to figure it all out," Sarah asked, clearly frustrated with me.

"I just want to know when you are going to be here," I offered weakly. That was the best I could do. I didn't know why I couldn't be more flexible, why I couldn't just go with the flow. Going with the flow, being laid back, leaving things up in the air? It's too scary.

Later she called to apologize.

"I'm sorry. I didn't mean to get mad at you. I guess you just need to plan things out and that's OK."

I felt a surge of relief because she understood something that I couldn't communicate.

"Yeah, it makes me feel more comfortable knowing when I'm going to see you. And that we planned it. So I don't have to be like, 'When am I going to see my sister? I miss her so much.'"

For me, calling and reiterating that we had plans that were set in place brought me the calm I needed in order to function. I felt the same way about Chris and knowing when he would get home from work.

"If you're not home that's OK, but I need to know around what time to expect you," I would explain to him.

People might see that as controlling. Part of it is unhealthy, yes, but a part of me just needed to plan more in order to feel safe. I even had to be picky about who my friends were because I couldn't handle having people misunderstand me. I was not trying to be naggy, even though it came across as being naggy. It just comforted me to feel more prepared, and it was what I needed to do at that point in time.

I realized that I had a problem and I had acknowledged that I wanted to change, but I still resisted asking for help. While it was a breakthrough for me to be honest about the state of my emotions and to admit that I needed help, it would take more courage to actually seek that help out. I still wanted to fix things on my own. I wanted to control my healing process, but that wasn't happening. I still felt nervous that I was going to appear weak and irrational. I didn't want to share how I was feeling except with Chris or some members of my family. But just as with the panic attacks, God would bring me to a place where I would have to seek the help I needed.

SECTION FOUR

Searching

But the Lord stood at my side and gave me strength.

2 Timothy 4:17

22

Rock Bottom

I was not feeling well, but it was more than just a physical sickness. I felt sick in every part of my body, from the inside out. I couldn't stop crying. A sadness was gripping me so tightly that I didn't think I would ever be able to shake it. My head was throbbing and my eyes were swollen almost to the point of being shut. But the most distressing part was the fact that I didn't know why this was happening.

"Chris, I need help," I managed to say between sobs as he walked in the front door after work. He dropped everything and walked over to the couch where I had been lying for hours. One look at me and he wrapped his arms around me, which only made me cry harder.

"I would rather die today than live my life not knowing when I am going to die because I am so afraid of death," I blurted out. I could feel his body stiffen against mine. "How am I going to die? Am I going to suffer? I just want to know that I am going to die tomorrow or next week and that it's over and I don't have to worry or wonder about it."

"Karin, you don't want that," Chris said wrapping his arms around me tighter.

"I know that I don't want that for real, but right now I just don't feel normal. I just feel like I am not myself and these thoughts and feelings are so out of control. I am not manic or suicidal—just very far off from who I know I am. I know that we just got married and I should be happy, but I'm not. I feel guilty that I am not a better wife. And I know that I said I want to be a mom, but I don't. I don't want kids. I do not want to bring a baby into this world when it is so painful and there is so much trauma and heartache. Why would we want to create another life when you know that they may die or you might die and life is filled with so much pain?"

Chris didn't say anything. He knew that there was nothing to say that would help me right then. We just lay on the couch together as I cried.

"I need help," I said again after my sobs had subsided a bit.

"I know," said Chris. "We'll get you the help you need."

We stayed on the couch, wrapped in each other's arms, until exhaustion made us fall asleep. Only then did I stop crying.

The next day, Chris stopped me in the hall to talk to me.

"I'm scared because you didn't make sense last night," he told me. "I didn't realize how bad it is for you, how much it is consuming you." Even though I had vocalized my pain, I had been hiding from everyone just how thoroughly my anxiety was impacting my life, even from my husband. I was scared to truly let people know how bad it was, for fear that they would judge me or reject me or worse, try to help me in ways that would just aggravate the problem. But feeling like I wanted to die scared me worse than feeling possibly rejected. It was the lowest I had ever felt and I was determined to never feel that way again.

The difference in my emotions from the first year after the crash to the second was shocking to me. The first year felt like it was all about life. *I'm alive, I survived,* I told myself time after time. "God is so good, isn't God amazing?" I would say to anyone who would listen. The reality of what we had been through hadn't hit me yet. It may have come earlier had I not gotten engaged and become busy planning the wedding before the year was over.

I'm going to be married. We're going to have kids and live happily ever after, I told myself. And I set about making it happen. It was a joyful and exciting year. After all, we were survivors who had our lives ahead of us. We were going to be married. We were planning a wedding. We were celebrating life.

The second year came crashing down on me and my focus changed from celebrating life to being consumed with death; my death, how I was going to die, how it felt for others to die. There was still life going on around me, but I couldn't celebrate it. A short time into the second year after the crash, my sister Sarah announced that she and her husband were going to have a baby, and my response to this good news surprised me.

I felt torn.

Sarah and I had always been close and while I had always had a desire to be a mom, the emotional turmoil of the crash had led me to believe that it is a selfish and irresponsible thing to have children.

"Why would she have a baby? Why would she want to bring a life into this world? Doesn't she realize how much pain there is in the world? Does she want her baby to experience that?" I ranted as Chris and I drove home one night. Being his logical self, he gave me several good and logical reasons for having kids, but I didn't want to hear them. Why anyone would want to bring a life into this broken-down, dangerous world that is full of trauma, risks and death was beyond me. It just seemed selfish. Even though I love my sister dearly and a part of me was excited about being an aunt, I couldn't help but feel upset at her decision. It seemed foolish and too risky. And I realized that this was not a normal response to such wonderful news, especially for me, someone who loved children so much.

My sister and I spoke often. Sarah had called to check up on me. I recall asking, "Aren't you afraid something is going to happen to your child? Aren't you afraid that you might die and not be able to take care of them?"

"No," she said, after a brief moment of silence. There was a peace in her voice that I longed for. "God is faithful. He'll take care of us."

I realized that my worry was based in fear, but also that I was jealous. I was not jealous of her ability to have children; I probably had the ability myself. I was jealous of her courage. I knew that I was not brave enough to have a baby right then.

Ever since I was a child I had wanted to have babies. When I was in kindergarten and we had what the teachers called "free play," where we could simply play with toys and friends, I usually chose to play house. But one day I decided to pretend that I was pregnant and that my friend was the nurse. I put a baby doll in my shirt. Very quickly our teacher came over and told me that we were not allowed to play pregnancy. I was sad at first, but I quickly perked up when I realized we could still play "mommy."

That wasn't the only time that I had shown an affinity for babies. My mom loves to tell the story about when I was two years old and we were at a store and a baby, who Mom says was not much younger than me, started crying in our aisle. Mom says I walked right over to the baby and said with complete confidence, "Shh, baby, it's OK. . . . Don't cry!"

When I got older, I loved to help in the nursery at church. While all the other kids were playing together I was always holding the newest baby at our church. And when I finally realized that I had met the man of my dreams, I couldn't wait to have children with him.

All that changed after the crash. I become afraid of everything, even something that I had wanted since before I could remember. I was afraid that it might get ripped away from me and the pain of losing it was not enough to warrant the joy of having.

My sister was doing something that I had always wanted to do, something that I was currently too fearful to attempt, and I didn't know how to handle that.

23

Reaching Out

It is God's providence that we were living in Colorado Springs during this time. He knew exactly where I needed to be during this vulnerable time. After too many months of insisting that I was fine, I was ready to admit that I was not. What's more, I was ready to accept help.

I don't know why it took me so long to admit it or to reach out for help. Maybe it was pride. Maybe I really did think that I could handle it on my own. Maybe I felt stupid for feeling so emotional so long after the incident. It most likely was a combination of all those things and more. Looking back, I can see that my need for help developed long before I admitted it, but hindsight is 20/20.

I finally realized that what I was feeling was much heavier than I was able to deal with on my own, but this realization did not come easily. It was only with Chris's insistence that I began to seek professional help.

"Karin, you really aren't doing well," he told me one day. "I can tell. It's OK to ask for help and I think you should."

When I called Denise, my mentor, she encouraged me to seek help as well.

Denise had been involved in my mom's Bible study at my church when I was younger. In high school I used to do childcare for the Bible study and Denise took an interest in me because

I was watching her daughters. Denise and I would always talk about fashion and style, and even though she was much older than I was, I felt that she could be a friend. A few months after I started watching her daughters she asked if we could have more intentional time together in a mentor relationship. I had never had a mentor before and I was intrigued.

We began meeting once a month and she and I would just share about our lives. My parents had recently taken me out of public school to homeschool me. As I have mentioned, this was upsetting to me because I had wanted to stay in public school. When I would rant and rave about how unfair it was, Denise was really great at listening to me and helping me process the changes in my life. I didn't feel I could confide in my mom regarding my feelings about that situation and I needed someone to talk to. Denise became my go-to person whenever I had something difficult to deal with. She would offer me advice about my relationships and help me make decisions about school and work. Later on she was my sounding board as I dealt with my desire to be engaged.

Most of our relationship could be summed up in one way: Denise challenging me to ask God "about the work He is currently doing in my life," and how can I join Him. She loves Jesus and always encourages me to make Him the focus of my life. I have never felt judged in her presence, only loved and accepted. She has called me out when I am not seeking God's will. She has challenged me to do things I was not ready to do.

So when Denise as well as Chris suggested I get help, I knew that I had no other choice.

I began to look for counselors and a good Christian counseling office. I could not have picked a better place to do this. I didn't have a lot of distractions because I was still new to Colorado Springs and so I began counseling with a willing spirit and plenty of time, albeit with some trepidation. My isolation in Colorado Springs had given me more free time to spend with Chris and with God, but it also gave me more time to think about the events on the Hudson and that wasn't necessarily a good thing, in my book.

Every day I went to work, to the gym and home. I also had a weekly appointment with my counselor. When I would get home, I would sleep because I was tired, but also because it kept me from thinking too much. When I came down with mono, I took it as a sign that my body was telling me to calm down and rest.

Chris was incredibly gracious to me during this time. I felt guilty about not being a more active and engaged wife, but no amount of guilt could get me up out of bed. I felt emotionally exhausted from the year I kept my emotions inside and it was manifesting itself physically now.

I found a job at Hope & Home, a foster care agency for children in Colorado Springs, and again, Jesus demonstrated that His plan and His timing are perfect. He knows what is to come. It was such a blessing to work there because they understand trauma and they let me go to counseling whenever I needed to, which was often.

* * *

"Are you really so worried about dying, Karin?" Chris asked me one day over dinner.

"I'm not worried about being dead. I'm glad that I get to go to heaven. I'm worried about *how* I'll die," I clarified. "And how it will feel, like, how badly will it hurt?" My worries seemed to be only increasing.

I thought about a story I recently saw on the news about a man who was dragged to death behind a truck and it made me feel faint. I wondered how he felt right before he died. I wondered how his family was coping without him. I wondered what was going through his mind. I couldn't seem to separate myself from his story and other similar news stories. They were beginning to haunt me.

Although my initial counselor was kind and compassionate, after months of meeting nothing seemed to be changing for me. I was still anxious all the time and I was still obsessed with death. I knew that I couldn't continue living my life in a constant state of fear, but I saw no end in sight.

24

EMDR

So many questions kept going through my mind about the day of the crash. For example, the way the day of the flight, our gate and the flight time were changed, which ended up being God's provision—but I wondered why He didn't simply have our flight cancelled or why He didn't move the birds out of the way of the engines.

I wondered what we would have done if the ice had been there on the river. What would have happened if we had taken off later or earlier? What if we had been flying lower or higher? What if the back doors had been opened? I would never get answers to my questions and I knew that I was not entitled to them, but they still plagued me.

All of these little pieces had to fall into place for us to be able to land on the river without dying and without killing others, little things that I had no idea about until after the whole thing was over. God was present and He was watching out for us.

I could see God's hand of provision all across that day and yet I still wondered why He didn't simply take over and prevent the crash. I thought a lot about how we don't understand the reasons behind things. We ask, "Why now? Why me? Why this?" But that's when we need to trust God. We should be comforted to believe that *He* knows, which is why we don't have to.

When I thought about the flight I imagined God in heaven looking down on us and saying "Ferries, get ready," "Birds, start flying." He orchestrated those things to happen. That gave me peace. He orchestrated them in a way that was perfect. Why? I believe that it was both for His greater good and for ours.

I was wrestling with how to live day to day trusting in God's power and God's ability to care for me. How could I avoid being so focused on what I can and cannot do and allow God to be in control?

Some days I felt I couldn't watch or hear of another event. Eventually I set up better boundaries in regards to my attention to the news, yet at times I was still too intrigued. I guess I thought that if I faced my fears I could overcome them sooner. I just had to figure out how to bring God into those things. How could I let my fears lead me closer to Him instead of pushing me further away from Him?

Even though I eventually moved on from my first counselor, she did pave the way for me to embrace the healing process and that changed the way that I felt about my anxiety and obsession with death. She showed me the Scripture that tells us to love God with all that you have and to love others as yourself:

> Jesus replied: "Love the Lord your God with all your heart and with all your soul and with all your mind." This is the first and greatest commandment. And the second is like it: "Love your neighbor as yourself." (Matthew 22:37–39)

She summed up those words with these: "Love yourself in such a way that you have something else to love others with." That was good for me to hear because I was struggling with the fact that my anxiety took so much of my energy that I didn't have time to invest in others. I felt guilty for not being a better wife, sister, daughter and friend. I felt selfish for not spending more time with others or doing more besides sleeping. Everything was making me feel that I was not good enough, that there was something seriously wrong with me.

My counselor helped me realize that I was allowed to take time for myself and that if I wanted to get to a place where I might have more energy to love others, I needed to take care of me first. I realized that if I didn't take care of myself, there would be no way I could be an effective wife or friend, because you can't pour into others if you yourself are empty.

I don't know if I would have pursued the treatment option that proved to be the most effective if my first counselor had not helped me to see that it was in everyone's best interest for me to take the time I needed to heal.

* * *

When someone suggested I try Eye Movement Desensitization and Reprocessing (EMDR), I jumped right in. Regular counseling hadn't yielded the results that I had hoped for and, although it helped to talk with someone about how I was feeling, I was growing impatient with the process. I didn't feel as if I were getting significantly better and I was desperate to see any kind of improvement.

I did not know much about EMDR when I began, but that didn't bother me. I had cautiously dipped my toe in the talk-therapy counseling world and it didn't work. Now, true to my nature, I was ready to dive in headfirst, ready to do whatever it took to yield some results. This in and of itself was a sign that I was doing a little better.

I saw my new EMDR counselor for two and a half months and it changed my life. He diagnosed me with a case of

Post-Traumatic Stress Disorder (PTSD), which came as a shock to me. I thought that the only people who had PTSD were the ones who had been through war or traumatic events where people had actually *died*. Since no one had died in the plane crash, I somehow thought I didn't qualify. I guess I was wrong.

My counselor was not a believer, which initially caused me to be hesitant because my struggles were so tied into my faith and I didn't think I could separate one from the other. I needed to be myself if I was going to get better and being myself meant being a Christian. I knew that it would take a mighty act of God to help heal me and therefore I wanted a Christian counselor. But our insurance covered EMDR, whereas it didn't cover the Christian counselor I had tried initially. So I pushed ahead and told my EMDR counselor about my faith. He was kind and patient.

With the realization that I could no longer afford *not* to work through my issues, I decided to believe that God could work through anyone. I felt desperately confident that this was the way to go. He didn't ask me to hide my faith. In fact, he affirmed it, which was a relief to me. He allowed me to assess myself, guiding me through the process.

What I saw wasn't pretty. I was a mess—a big, emotional, unstable mess. I knew that I was, but until I stopped and actually laid out my issues like a picnic lunch, I did not realize just how deep my hurt had gone.

My EMDR counselor phrased it in a way that resonated with me: "You're in a car and there's a huge mountain outside your window," he tells me during one of our sessions. "The mountain is your plane crash and all that you experienced. Right now, all you can see is how big the mountain is. It's daunting. But you'll keep driving each and every day. As time goes on, the crash will become a memory. You will be able to identify it in the distance, but it won't be a huge mountain right next to you. It won't be so consuming. It won't be all that you see."

I understood his metaphor and it helped put things in perspective, but honestly, I just wanted to be past it. I knew that I needed to take the time to work through my emotions and to heal, but sometimes I wished I could just snap my fingers and be over it. I knew that down the road I would get past my mountain and the crash would be a smaller part of my life, a memory that would no longer be so overwhelming, but I wanted that day to be *this* day.

25

Big Picture

I only knew one small piece of the whole when we crashed. Each person on that plane went through a similar experience and we each walked away changed, but in different ways. We only knew what we had been through and although we could relate to one another, none of us had the very same experience. For my part, I knew that something was wrong with the plane and that I needed to pray. That was my piece that I was responsible for, but the whole picture was that we had hit the birds and we were going to crash into the river. I didn't know everything, and that was for the best. I couldn't have handled the whole picture. I knew what I was supposed to do and that was enough.

I can see this as a theme in my life: not knowing the whole picture, but being able to see how God works through my situations.

I see this with my relationship with Chris. I didn't know why God called him to Colorado Springs for work, and when he first went it was difficult for me to be in a long-distance relationship, but that was just a piece of the whole picture. I didn't like it when it meant moving away from my circle of friends in Boulder once we were married. Now, however, I see the blessings that stemmed from him moving. God knew that I would need to be in Colorado Springs in order to get the help I needed after the crash.

There are many, many things today that I don't understand. I don't see their purpose and I tend to get frustrated or discouraged by them, but then I remind myself that I only know a small piece. God knows the whole. I don't understand how everything is going to work, but God does and so I don't have to understand. It isn't my job to figure out how all the pieces fit together. If God only gives me a little glimpse, I have to live in that and trust that He knows best. And honestly, it is best that I don't know because my frail mind can't handle knowing too much.

Take, for instance, an afternoon that we spent in New York before the crash. While exploring Liberty Island, the topic of swimming in the cold water arose. Made to evacuate the island because an abandoned stroller had been found and everyone was still on high alert because of 9/11, we were boarding the ferry, feeling nervous, and my mind started to spin.

"Chris, what if the ferry sank?" I asked out of nowhere as we pulled away from the island. Big chunks of ice were floating past us, looking like mini icebergs.

"We wouldn't make it. We'd be way too cold. We'd probably die of frostbite," he told me, making me feel more uneasy than I had. I wished that I hadn't asked.

If I had known the big picture, if I had known somehow that we were going to crash, I wouldn't have boarded that plane. I wouldn't have gone to New York in the first place. I would have thought that we were going to die when we crashed. And if I hadn't experienced the plane crash I would have missed out on a life-changing and faith-changing season of life.

SECTION FIVE

Learning

What is to give light must endure burning.

Viktor E. Frankl[4]

26

Catastrophizing

People often ask me how the crash has changed me and that is a difficult question to answer. It's funny because usually the first thing that pops to mind when I am asked that question is the fact that in my life pre-crash, I shopped a lot. I enjoyed fashion, I enjoyed shopping and I enjoyed looking good. I didn't have an unhealthy obsession with my looks, but I did put a lot of time and money into my appearance. I have been told on many occasions that I have an uncanny resemblance to Reese Witherspoon and I kind of enjoy that. As I mentioned, right before we got on the plane I wondered whether or not I should get a pedicure. Although pedicures and pampering aren't inherently bad, I think I used to put too much stock in that type of thing.

Immediately following the crash I made a complete change. My interests changed and seemed to be in direct conflict with what they were before. It is as if my interests were on a swinging pendulum, they became so far removed from what they were before. I lost the ability to enjoy treats and luxuries because the fatalistic part of me wondered if I would even be around to enjoy them long-term. I began questioning everything and wondering if anything truly matters or if we are just biding our time here on Earth. I developed a lot of catastrophizing thoughts where I saw the worst in any and every situation. I became unhealthy in my approach to money in that I felt I needed to save as much as possible just in case some disaster might strike.

I knew that God had provided for me and Chris, but there was still a part of me that felt I was simply killing time before some other disaster would hit. It was as though I was at the surface gasping for breath before being pulled under again. I had escaped death once, but I seriously doubted I would be able to do it again. I found myself trying to bank time, preparing for a catastrophe. What kind of catastrophe, I didn't know, but I felt sure that one was just around the corner. I began to see disaster all around me in places where I had previously been happily and foolishly oblivious.

I was having a hard time living and enjoying the blessings God had given me because I was so focused on whether these things actually matter. When I die, would it matter that Chris and I got new couches rather than keeping our old ones? In the end would it matter if Chris and I had a great retirement or not? Would we even be around to enjoy retirement together?

I was wrestling with issues that people don't really think about because they feel like they are immortal. I *knew* I'm not, in spite of cheating death. *In the end,* I would think, *what really matters?*

Before the crash, I thought I was invincible. Don't we all when we are young? The crash made me realize how foolish that was. I feel like I got burned by my own optimism, as if I should have had a more realistic view of the world. Thus I began a futile attempt at trying to protect myself from unknown catastrophes, constantly preparing for the worst. By "preparing," I mean anticipating the worst thing that could happen in any given scenario.

The more the people in my life tried to help me, the more isolated I felt. They would say something meant to encourage me, but it would have the opposite effect. I bought into this lie that I was the only one who had experienced something so traumatic and began to reject people because they just didn't seem to understand. It was foolish of me and frankly, a little arrogant, to believe that I was the only one who had experienced trauma in my life.

I realize now that most people have deep wounds that they carry around with them, their own "plane crashes," so to speak. Chances are it isn't a literal plane crash. Let's be honest. That's pretty rare. But the more I shared my story, the more people shared their experiences with trauma. People shared their stories of loss and death and crisis and even though each event was different, the emotional reactions that they had were similar.

I realize now more than ever that life is difficult and that no one really escapes unscathed. God didn't promise us a life without trials. But He *did* promise that He is *for* us, so nothing can stand against us:

> If God is for us, who can be against us? . . . I am convinced that neither death nor life, neither angels nor demons, neither the present nor the future, nor any powers, neither height nor depth, nor anything else in all creation, will be able to separate us from the love of God that is in Christ Jesus our Lord. (Romans 8:31, 38–39)

I can draw confidence from knowing that God is for me, no matter what trials lie ahead.

27

Death

Chris thought we were going to die. When he saw the water through our porthole, his first thought was, "We're not getting out alive."

I was convinced that we were going to back to the airport for an emergency landing. The thought of death didn't cross my mind until after we had landed and the water came rushing in. Chris was sitting right next to me the whole time and he knew that we were going into the water. He had seen footage of other planes landing on water and knew that we would topple and most likely perish as our plane was ripped apart in the crash. We lived the exact same moment, but we lived it thinking two different things.

When our plane hit the river and I saw the cabin filling with water, I thought we were going to drown, trapped in a giant metal coffin. Chris thought, "We're alive. The plane is intact. We're going to survive." We flip-flopped our mind-sets. I ended in a state of trauma; physiologically, my body felt like we were going to die. He ended on a high note of, "We're going to live!" I think this might be why I have struggled more than Chris, because I landed thinking we were going to die. Chris landed and felt relief knowing that we were going to make it since we had made it through the landing. We ended on such different notes.

I know of one fellow passenger who would not fly for a year after the crash, but most of the people on our flight had to take the same flight over and over again because of work. I have never asked the other passengers if anyone else has struggled as I have. Perhaps they have and they just haven't talked about it. Sometimes it has seemed like I am the only one who is struggling the way that I am out of 155 people, so my struggle feels isolating. I have to guard against that.

Naturally other people didn't always know that I was going through this; therefore I had to be proactive about protecting myself. On the outside, I looked like a normal person who had her life together. Inside, I was a mess. I didn't have physical scars from what I experienced, but the emotional scars were deep and were not yet healed.

It isn't natural to live in such a constant state of fear. I was scared of the pain and suffering of dying. I was afraid of missing out on my life because of death, but I was also afraid that my fear was already making me miss out on life. If I had a baby and then died I figured that that Chris would probably remarry and, as selfish as it is, I didn't want him to remarry because I was afraid that he would forget me. I wanted to be married to him and I wanted to grow old with him. I wished not to have these thoughts, but I had to learn how to embrace them. Stuffing them didn't do any good.

The fact of the matter is that I could have died at the age of twenty-four without getting to marry to love of my life or grow old with him. I sometimes wondered if anything that I did before the crash really mattered. I really questioned whether my life would have had any impact if I had died at twenty-four. Would I have left a legacy or would my life have been too short to really make a difference? I wanted to live a long life and I didn't want to live it thinking this way! I was scared that desires of my heart would not come to fruition—life-changing things like having kids and also simple things like going on vacation.

One of the passages of Scripture that was important to my healing is Isaiah 61. This passage talks about being anointed to preach the good news to the poor. It also adds, "He has sent me to bind up the brokenhearted, to proclaim freedom for the captives and release from darkness for the prisoners" (Isaiah 61:1). That is what I wanted: freedom and release from darkness. God wants to give freedom to those who don't believe in him. He wants me, and all of us, to be whole and out of the darkness. But there is a lot of work involved with this. Not work to earn your salvation, but rather, work to become more like Christ.

In counseling, resting and reflecting, I was doing the work I thought needed to be done, but things weren't getting better. The work that I needed to do required me to release control into God's hands, to trust in His timing and to bless the season I was in. That was hard, because it felt like inaction, which I don't like. I like quick fixes so that I can be done and move on. This wasn't going to be a quick fix, though, and that was becoming more and more evident.

28

Relationships

The plane crash changed me in every aspect of my life including relationships. While the crash served as a good catalyst for my relationship with Chris, it also became a wedge in some of my other relationships.

It wasn't that my friends didn't care about me. They loved me. But I was not able to be truly honest with them about how I was feeling. Vulnerability was just another thing that I was afraid of. Therefore, they didn't quite know how to respond to my sudden change in behavior. I am sure that it caught them by surprise.

The first year came and went and I seemed fine. I laughed, I smiled, I freely spoke about our experience and (because I ignored my feelings about the crash) it didn't seem to affect me. The second year came and I fell apart. I was a mess, and I felt that people didn't care about what I had been through anymore. Intellectually I knew that wasn't true. To me however, I felt that people were thinking, "Oh, it happened a year ago. She's probably fine."

But I was anything but fine. I was depressed. I was scared. I was feeling worse than I ever had before. And to top it all off, I felt like my friends just didn't get it.

My resentment for the people I called my friends grew until one day when I finally sat them down and had an honest conversation.

"I am not doing well," I said over lunch, a revelation that surprised them all because I had been so good at acting like I was fine. "I need you to ask me how I am doing and I realize that this is coming a lot later than it should, but this is what I need from you."

Their loving response gave me the confidence to open up more in the future, but it wasn't as easy as I had hoped it would be.

Another factor that made my relationships so hard to maintain was that so many of my friends were in exciting places in their lives, and I was not. When my best friend in Colorado Springs became engaged, I tried to be happy for her. I knew I should be and I truly wanted to be, but my emotional state made it difficult to celebrate anything. The more people shared their good news with me, the more I began to feel like what I was going through wasn't legitimate or worthwhile. Everyone else was in a really great, happy place and I was in such a dark place, so something must be wrong with me, right? *What is wrong with me that I can't be happy for my friends?*

There were many times that I didn't want to share what I was going through because I didn't want to rain on someone else's parade, so I kept my feelings to myself. This started a continuing spiral of falling into a darker and darker place. Every time I was around people I felt that my depression took away from their happiness. I began to feel as if people no longer want me around since I couldn't muster the same enthusiasm as everyone else. *I probably wouldn't want me around either.*

I knew that I was projecting my feelings onto them, which wasn't fair, but at the same time I thought about how hard it is to predict when someone who has experienced something awful will be "better." For example, someone who has lost their child doesn't stop grieving at any point in their life. Their friends may think, "You shouldn't feel your emotions as strongly as you did in the beginning. I know it's hard, but it's been three years." What people don't understand is that three years after a traumatic event can be the hardest season because a person might just then be beginning their journey toward healing.

My struggle made it difficult for me to reach out and say, "I'm not doing well. I don't need you to fix it; I just need you to be here for me." I felt that everyone else's lives must be perfect, as crazy as it seems. I also couldn't shake the idea, *I just got married. I should be happy. I shouldn't be struggling.*

I had to become more careful about who I would allow in my life. I needed people who could support me. I had to learn to speak up and tell people what I needed and not expect them to "just know." It wasn't fair to just expect others, Chris included, to comprehend my mental and emotional state.

I was once a bundle of energy. I could do a variety of activities each day. I could go to coffee, I could go to work, I could work out and then go home and do even more. I thrived on action. Now, I felt completely depleted of energy. I had to prioritize and choose one activity over another. I had to decide between cleaning the house and working out because I just couldn't do both anymore. It made me wonder if I would ever have enough energy to live the kind of life I wanted to again.

A few months into my search for professional help, a dear friend of mine lost her baby. It was traumatic for her, which wasn't surprising. What *was* surprising was how hard I took her loss. I immediately recognized that my weird overly emotional response was tied into my unresolved feelings about the plane crash. This was the first big traumatic event that had happened to someone I loved following the crash and I was unprepared for navigating this unfamiliar territory.

Well, Karin, hang on and do your best, was the best pep talk I could manage for myself. That was hardly instructive or comforting.

It did make me realize that I had been left with a heightened sensitivity to other people's trauma. Even though their trauma might be very different from my own, the feelings that go along with trauma were often so similar that I did not have a hard time identifying with them. Somehow, when others are grieving, something got triggered in me. The pain that I felt for them got jumbled in with the remnants of the pain I felt in connection to the crash until they were so tangled that I had a hard time deciphering one from the other.

It made me a real joy to be around sometimes.

It's easy for people who haven't experienced loss to move on and think that people are over their suffering, but that isn't always the case. Oftentimes, people hurt and grieve and process for years before they are able to feel healed. And when you go through something as traumatic as losing a child, I don't know that you ever fully heal. I think that you simply realize that life goes on, but that you always carry that pain with you.

You can't see emotional scars. A perfectly healthy-looking individual may be a mess of memories and fears on the inside. Others cannot tell what's going on inside and no one can anticipate what's going to trigger someone's memories. I couldn't live in fear of my emotions or when they were going to gurgle up, especially when other people's trauma triggered my own trauma.

As one of the scarred, walking around whole on the outside but broken on the inside, I felt that I had been given the gift of perspective. I could be sensitive to people and what was causing them to feel their sadness and loss again. Two different people might have both lost their parents when they were young, but what causes them to feel their loss again might be completely different. I have learned that you don't know what is going to set someone off and you can't always avoid it, but you can be sensitive to how people respond to you.

The road of a friend or family member can be a hard one to navigate. Many times I remember going to bed before the sun had even set and not waking up again until late the next day because I was so exhausted from processing. I would have expected Chris to say something like, "Well, you're boring. We just got married and you just want to sleep all day," but he never said that to me. He didn't have an agenda or a timeline for me to follow. The fact that he has been so mellow and relaxed has, in some ways, given me permission to really dig into this healing process. When I feel like I should be over this, but Chris shrugs and says, "This is just where you are."

Not too long after my friend lost her baby, I had another friend die unexpectedly and again, I reacted in a way I had not anticipated. My reaction was intense and I was not able to hide it from my husband.

"Why are you so upset about this?" Chris asked, when I hadn't been able to function properly in many days. "I mean, I know that you are sad, but this seems to go beyond the normal sadness. I didn't know the two of you were *that* close."

"Because there's no guarantee in life," I told him. "You do not know when you will die."

The uncertainty got to me. I couldn't seem to stop crying. My reactions were visceral. While I was grieving for others, I was also aware that I was grieving for myself; for my loss of innocence concerning my immortality and for the life that I was missing out on because of my crippling emotional state. For days on end, I cried at random times. There was a raw, deep grief in me that had gained more power during the months I had suppressed it, and it seemed determined to come out.

It was like emotional vomit. I had held it back for as long as I could and now we were at the point of no return. There was no stopping it or containing it. All self-control had gone out the window.

29

Don't Trump My Trauma

People always say that it is better to feel empathetic than sympathetic and I am here to tell you that they are wrong. I know what extreme empathy feels like and it stinks. Once my empathy level skyrocketed, I could no longer hear of any disaster and simply think, "Oh, my goodness, that's so sad," and then move on with my life. No, now I became fixated on the ramifications of tragedies. When I heard about a disaster, whether from a friend or on the news, my mind started to work overtime. Then I began to develop panic attacks. They were triggered by any kind of bad news, personal or otherwise. Bad news sent my brain into overdrive and inevitably pushed me over the edge of anxiety until I developed a full-blown panic attack.

What does this mean for all the people impacted by this disaster? I asked myself when I heard about any sort of tragedy involving death. *How does this tragedy affect the rest of the world and how might it change my life?* For the life of me, I couldn't seem to separate myself from the pain that I heard about on the news, and I couldn't compartmentalize, either. I knew that those tragedies couldn't reach me and yet I still agonized over them.

Most people feel sad about an event or loss, but then move on if it does not personally affect them. I couldn't make myself do that anymore. I personalized everything. I knew I was doing it; I just didn't know how to fix it. It's not like I *wanted* to be all emotional because of the heartache in the world. I would have liked to be able to hear a news story and not think twice about it, but I could not.

How could I learn how to think and feel and do what God wanted me to do? Maybe this new level of empathy was helpful, but the steps to recovery seemed unclear. Surely this was not the end point, right? I suspected that God was giving me the gift of empathy in order to love and relate to others, but I needed to learn how to use it without letting it consume me.

I had to be careful not to think so pessimistically about the world around me. It was unrealistic to think that I would be able to live in the hunky-dory, God-is-so-good world as I did the first year after the crash. But I did need to realize that this event and these emotions were going to deepen my faith.

One of the positive parts of being in the plane crash was the way I could now put myself in others' shoes. I never glossed over their pain. I felt it with them. I internalized it and I tried to identify with it. I did not see their pain as separate from my life because I had known pain myself. I took it all in. I remember what it was like to have people hear my story and then gloss over it as if it was no big deal. I can't count how many times I've been asked to share our story only to be inter-rupted by other people's stories about plane crashes they've heard about.

"Did you hear about this…?" They'll ask, before I've even finished talking.

"Please don't try to trump my trauma when I've shared this really traumatic event with you," I always want to say to them, but instead I just sit and nod. I want them to acknowledge my trauma, at least, before they jump into their own stories. It's not hard to say, "Oh, that must be so difficult for you," instead of asking immediately if I've heard about this or that.

I remember an instance that occurred in March after the plane crash. We went up to a cabin with one of my former roommates and her husband. A bunch of people came along for the trip that we didn't know. While we were sitting at the dinner table the subject of the plane crash came up. People were naturally curious and began asking us a variety of questions. And again, we didn't mind sharing, but we weren't offering up much information when they asked us questions. I didn't mind their curiosity, but sometimes their questions felt more like prying.

There was one guy who kept staring at me as we were sitting there and he was making me uncomfortable. After we had answered a number of questions, he suddenly blurted out, "Gosh, I would have loved to have been the person who got to open the window of the plane to let people escape."

The room got silent and I could feel the color drain from my face. The rest of the group moved on to another topic, but I couldn't move past his remark. *Seriously?* I inwardly fumed. *What are you thinking? Why would you ever say that? Why would you wish to be in a plane crash?* I realized that because we had all survived, people assumed that it was an easy thing to experience, but it wasn't. What he didn't realize is that the crash didn't happen beautifully and smoothly. Yes, we all lived, but there was panic, chaos and the threat of death before we were rescued.

Sometimes people are just insensitive. I tried to understand that. When that guy spoke out of turn, I just thought, *You are such an idiot. Why would you want to go through that?* He was assigning a sense of adventure to our ordeal that didn't exist in the moment. It *wasn't* thrilling. It *wasn't* exciting. It was terrifying. He was seeing the trauma as a chance to do something heroic, but he couldn't know for sure how he would have acted in that situation and he also didn't know what kind of lasting effects that situation might have had on him. This would apply to any major trauma situation, from plane crashes to cancer to grief upon the loss of a loved one.

Learning how to empathize in a healthy way is not easy, even if you do it with good intentions. It is a struggle to empathize, but still to keep emotions in balance. Quite likely it is a process that takes a lifetime to learn.

30

Changing My Focus

God has been so good to Chris and me, and I want to live my life in a way that honors Him. We were in a plane crash and we didn't die! It still amazes me. It's humbling to know that God saved us. All my life, He has protected me and not just during that one instance on the Hudson. I am so grateful. I don't think we, as believers, can ever give God enough thanks for what he has done in our lives.

EMDR had helped me significantly, but I still had a way to go. I still thought about the pain and suffering of dying every time I heard about someone dying. If I didn't check myself, I would start to obsess over the pain. *Did they suffer?* I always wondered. I thought about the event of dying and what I would do if it were me in the same situation; I would personalize it. I would also think about those left behind, the families and the people affected by this person's death. *Will they be OK?* I always wondered.

I had been trying not to, but I still dwelt on bad events for way too long. They really shook me up. I became way too emotionally attached to people that I didn't even know simply because they had suffered loss. I was still preoccupied with death, not just my own, but death in general, asking the same questions that revolved around pain and how it physically feels to die. Of course not many answers were readily available to me.

The scariest point in the plane crash was when we were in the plane and I thought we were going to drown. Looking back, I still wondered, *Would I have passed out?* or *Would I have felt it?* What does it feel like when we die? Do we just go to sleep? Do we feel it? Personally, I just wanted to know that it was going to be fast. I just wanted to be with Jesus.

At my lowest point in this journey, I became preoccupied with the end times, the book of Revelation, and the timing of Jesus' return. To me, the timing of his return dictated whether or not I could handle being martyred if it came to that. I also wondered, *If Jesus comes back before I die, will I ever have to experience death?* I worried about living through the tribulation. It sounds crazy now and somewhat trivial, but these were real concerns to me. I dedicated many hours, weeks and months to worrying about these events. And I don't mean worrying in passing, on and off throughout the months. There were some days where it was all I could think about.

I really struggled with how we, as Christians, are supposed to live when we know that the end times are coming eventually, but without being consumed by thinking about the end. Two Scriptures brought me great comfort during this time. One was Mark 13:32 which reminds us that no one knows when Jesus is going to come back. ("But about that day or hour no one knows, not even the angels in heaven, nor the Son, but only the Father.") Even though this might not seem comforting, it helped me cope with the crazies who proclaimed that they knew exactly when the Rapture was going to happen.

Another verse that helped me was Proverbs 31:25, which reads: "She is clothed with strength and dignity; she can laugh at the days to come." It reminded me that I didn't have to worry about the future. I could actually laugh at the days to come because I was living under God's grace. It was convicting for me to realize that I could actually enjoy my life because God gave it to me to live abundantly. I clung to these verses and to God's promise to care for me.

I remembered what I had learned about how Christians were persecuted in the world and I wondered if I could endure that level of suffering. I had many, many tearful conversations with God explaining to him that I loved Him, but that I didn't think I could mentally or emotionally handle being crucified or stoned. For a few months, I even began to convince myself that the end times were upon us and that it was just a matter of days before we all were going to die. I remember driving to work, staring at Pike's Peak, feeling as though my life could be over at any minute. It was a panicky place to be. I felt a little as if I were drowning in my own worries and paranoia.

I remember driving home and praying, *God, I know that this world has sin in it and that we are sinful. We have You now and You've made it right. You gave us this world to enjoy. Yes, there are things that are bad and don't bring You glory. You created me to live on this earth and I can't condemn this earth and be mad about people and things. I can't deny the things you call blessings.* I struggled with doing this.

I clung to the hope that in the future I would be able to enjoy my life, living and trusting God with whatever He has planned for me. It would take time for me to balance life and death in my head and in my heart. I just wanted to have the kind of perspective that God wants me to have. I wanted to be able to enjoy what God had given me, to be a good steward of my money and my time and my life and my heart, all woven together—not be incapable of enjoying my life because of being so worried about losing it.

31

Glimpses of Redemption

God showed me glimpses of how He wanted to redeem what I had been through. In 2013, I got a phone call from Katie Couric asking me if I could fly out to New York to be on *Katie*, her talk show. We had only a week's notice and Chris could not get off work. Since I needed a flying buddy, I was able to get my sister to come with me. We knew the show was going to be about Heroes and that Captain Sully would be there. (Katie Couric wanted to do a segment honoring Captain Sully and the passengers whose lives he had saved, with special emphasis on how their lives had changes since the crash four years before. I brought with me my first child, Elaina, who was eight months old.)

We stayed at a nice hotel near Central Park, and we were in New York for less than forty-eight hours. It was a quick trip, for sure. Katie was very genuine. We had a few dry runs of our interview so I would know where to go and where to sit. I knew they were going to ask me about the plane crash, which was the whole reason for having me there. What I didn't know was that the crash was going to be linked to how it helped it advance my relationship with Chris. That was a bit of a surprise, but one that I felt I handled well.

I loved going and had such a great time getting my makeup done, reuniting with some of the other passengers and having some time with Sully and his family. It was so great to create another positive and life-giving experience with New York and flying. Each time I flew again and nothing happened, I could feel myself releasing a little more of the trauma of the crash.

Nowadays when we fly, Chris and I handle ourselves quite differently from each other. Chris doesn't usually tell people what we've been through. He doesn't think it is anyone's business and flying doesn't scare him. I, on the other hand, tell many people about the crash, especially the flight attendants. It's just good for them to know so that if I start to really freak out on a flight they know why. I also let them know so that they can check on me occasionally, especially if I am flying alone. This comes in handy, especially when there is turbulence. I can't tell you how many times I have been reassured that turbulence is normal by a kind flight attendant.

Flying is still scary for me and I think it always will be, but I am getting better. I have learned how to cope and I have a plan that I like to stick to. We always try to get flights that leave early in the morning so that I'm tired and not totally awake. I find it hard to fly with Chris because he just wants to look out the window and be quiet. He wants to listen to hear that everything's OK with the plane and I just want to talk. So I'll talk to the person next to me. I talk too much, probably, but I can't help it. When we fly and I see that people are fine and that things are normal with the plane I can relax, but only a little. Flying is far from normal for me. I have to remind myself that no one else is consumed with the worry that I experience and I shouldn't be either. I have defied the odds and have survived a plane crash. What are the odds that I would be in another one?

When I fly now I try to remind myself of the positives associated with travel. I think, "Now I'm creating new memories and new experiences. Those are the things that I can dwell on." I am working hard to replace my negative thoughts with hopeful thoughts about the future and not dreading what's to come.

Every time I fly, the question of *Is this normal?* is floating around in my head. It's comforting to me to be reassured that things really are all right and that there is nothing wrong with the plane. I don't know if I will ever be able to fly again without some sense of fear, but I am looking forward to the day when I can begin to fly like a normal person again.

One reason the crash was so difficult to work through is because it tested my relationship with God. I understood that this was something that God had allowed in my life, but I didn't understand why. It wasn't as if I had made the choice to be involved in a plane crash. God knew it was going to happen and He also knew that I was going to struggle. So why would a loving God allow me to suffer? Isn't that a question we ask over and over again? I don't think I have *the* answer, but I have arrived at some conclusions that sit well with me.

God lovingly allows challenges into my life to help me grow. It isn't something He does *to* me. And I have a choice about how I'm going to respond to whatever circumstances I encounter. I don't have to play the victim. I can be an active player in my own life and choose how I respond. This is difficult for me because it usually means that the situation is beyond my control. But I *can* control my emotions and my response.

The question I ask myself specifically is: do I trust that God works in all of the details? Do I believe He will work for the good of those He loves? After the crash, people would say things like, "You just have to pray more, trust God, read your Bible."

I wanted to say, "I'm doing those things, but this is a lot to handle."

There have been times when I've been insensitive when other people have gone through difficult circumstances. Sometimes you just say, "God works for the good" because it's the best thing we know to say. I know I've done that. It's easier to believe God is working things together for good when it's something inconvenient, but relatively small, like your car breaking down. But what about when a baby is stillborn? Or a child is diagnosed with cancer? What about when a mom dies, a friend has chronic pain, a high school student tells her parents she's atheist, a spouse has an affair, your only car gets totaled? We have to ask ourselves: Do I believe now? Do I believe this experience is representative of all things and that good can come from it?

I struggle with that, but I have to hold on to God's Word. And He has been faithful. I also have to do some self-examination and reflection. Do I live my life as if I believe that principle? Am I looking for opportunities in everything, both happy and sad, to glorify Him? Or do I plan and prepare because I don't know how all things are going to work together?

The crash was a complete shock, obviously. I had no idea that we were crashing even as we were landing on the Hudson. Had I known, I would have been the crazy one on the plane. I would have screamed. I would have panicked. I don't think I could have handled it. God was protecting me from myself.

I was the one who bought the tickets for our trip and one of the main reasons I bought those exact tickets was because they were cheap. I've been asked by well-meaning strangers and friends if I feel guilty about what happened, as if we could have avoided everything if I had simply purchased other tickets. I don't feel guilty and the reason why is that I am convinced that there's a greater purpose for my life. There's more happening that I am aware of. I feel confident that God wanted me on that plane for a reason and I don't question that.

The Bible is full of verses that instruct us to trust in God. He is worthy of our trust. I claim that truth.

I am a part of His plan and I don't want to waste my life.

SECTION SIX

Growing

The real Son of God is at your side. He is beginning to turn you into the same kind of thing as Himself.

C.S. Lewis[5]

32

My Faith

The biggest impact of the crash has been on my faith. As believers, we know that we will face trials in this lifetime. (See James 1:2.) Somehow, however, we often believe that because we're Christians those trials won't be as hard or that somehow we'll just skip through them. If we look at history though, we can see that that simply isn't true. People of faith have had to suffer through so much.

My dad once said something that really stuck with me: A lot of people in other countries are persecuted for their faith, but in America we're not persecuted like other Christ-followers around the world, so God has to allow other events to happen for us to hit rock bottom in order to fully understand His love and faithfulness. I believe that God is faithful to do this for each and every one of us. It looks different for different people, but the end result—understanding God better—should be the same. For me, God just happened to do this in a really dramatic way.

Throughout everything, I can honestly say that I have never questioned my faith in God. I have always believed in His existence, but I *have* wrestled with His sovereignty and whether He actually cares for me as an individual. My limited human mind cannot comprehend how He can possibly hear and respond to all of our prayers, but I know that He does.

During some of my darkest months I started reading *Trusting God: Even When Life Hurts,* by Jerry Bridges. In his book, Bridges talks about the pain that we will inevitably suffer in life. He talks about how, through pain, we can get to know Jesus better and how God can use pain for good in our lives.

That book was really good for me. One of the themes of the book is about how God does not do anything that isn't for our good and that doesn't bring Him glory. I wrestled with that because at the time, that plane crash didn't feel good at all. But there have been so many good things that have come from it. I can see that now. I know now that it was showing God's power and glory. It showed His character. It showed that He is a protector and that He is faithful and that He is powerful. He is perfect.

Another theme of the book is that God sustains whatever He creates. I had to cling to the knowledge that I was God's creation, "fearfully and wonderfully made" (Psalm 139:14) and that He was going to sustain me. At times, it didn't feel like He was there. I felt abandoned and I wondered why He would allow me to suffer. I think we all feel that way sometimes, but that is when we have to cling to His promises.

I know I don't have a shallow relationship with God, but sometimes I find it difficult to be spiritual because I am struggling so much. I struggle because I feel like others might think that I am not spiritual enough to handle my experiences well. At the end of the day, praying and reading my Bible the way I want to feels too emotionally draining for me. There are times that I choose sleep over prayer and I feel guilty about it. But God knows where I am at and I trust that he will extend me grace.

It's easy to say that what happened on the Hudson that day was a miracle and many people have said it. But I want people to know that it was God's miracle. Yes, Sully had to fly the plane perfectly and it took incredible wisdom and skill on his part, but all the other factors that went into our safe landing can only be attributed to God. It was *His* miracle. He is all-knowing and all-powerful and He doesn't leave things up to chance.

It was not chance that we ended up in Colorado Springs. It's not chance that I've met the people I needed to meet to help me in my journey. There is evidence of God's master plan all over my life.

My faith isn't based on what makes sense. It's *faith*, a blind faith. I know from past experiences that God is faithful in providing for me and taking care of me and my needs. He has done it in the past, and not always in the way that I thought He should. My faith doesn't always make sense, but I am learning that faith doesn't guarantee knowledge.

God's sovereignty is something I have to work through as well. God only does things that are for my good or His glory. Sometimes it's hard to think, "OK, today is ultimately for His good even though it's difficult." I have to trust that He is sovereign, which isn't always easy for me.

I want to live my life with the knowledge that God is in control. We don't know what He is going to do, but that doesn't have to create fear in me. I don't have to be afraid of what God has in store for me. On the day of the plane crash, God gave me everything that I needed for that day to make it through and survive.

Looking back, I realize that God was giving me the words to pray when our plane was going down. He was giving me His words! I honestly believe that when we align our hearts with God, He gives us His words to pray. That day when I started praying, "God, lay this plane down gently," He knew what was going to happen even though I didn't have a clue. I had obviously never prayed a prayer like that before in my life!

I don't think that if I hadn't prayed those words that it would have changed anything, but I think that sometimes it's just so easy to pray what we want and not what God wants. How often do we sit down and say, "What matters to you, God? How do you want me to pray?" In that moment, I didn't know what was going on, but God gave me a gift in giving me the words to speak. God wanted that for me. That was his sovereignty.

A lot of research happened after the crash because we had defied all odds by surviving. I recently watched one of the many documentaries made about our experience. If the plane had been flying faster and the nose tipped higher, the wing probably would have broken upon impact causing immeasurable damage to the airplane and also to people. If it had been going slower with the nose facing down, the plane would have broken in half. The landing came together perfectly with the perfect speed and the perfect angle; it had to be precise and it was! Also, we had Captain Sully, who had been a pilot for over thirty years. He also had special training to be a glider pilot, and he also trained other people. He was the perfect person to land our plane without engine power.

Someone once made the comment, "It's just good people doing good things" in reference to our crash, but I disagree. Good people can't land planes. It does not matter how good Captain Sully was, because it was so much out of his control. There is so much evidence that God was part of all of this. He put Captain Sully in the cockpit. He placed those good, selfless people in our path that day.

More evidences of God's provision: The wind died down during our landing. Because of how the plane was floating once we landed, it kept bumping the ferries and each bump would push the plane down further into the water. If it had been as windy that day as it had been the whole weekend, the plane would have sunk much more quickly.

Another evidence of God's provision: Some people in the back tried to exit using the rear doors, but they wouldn't open. If they had opened, the plane would have sunk faster, giving us less time to be rescued. Another crucial detail: God made sure that the Hudson was empty of the boats that would normally have been all over the water—but that ferries and other rescue boats were close at hand. Nobody realized these small things at the time, but now we know about them because of the post-crash research. There's probably a lot more that we will never know. It goes to show that God knows what He's doing, and things don't happen by chance. God knows all of them. That's why, when I try to control everything, I know I'm not believing that God will care for me.

I get so stuck in the small details of life and wonder how things will work out. Why can't I remember the truth? It's not about the good feelings and being happy, but about knowing God more. It's not about good people and human capabilities. Even though Captain Sully was piloting our plane, God was in control.

33

My Family

Chris has been awesome and supportive throughout this whole time. He hasn't been to counseling because he doesn't need it, which is amazing to me. He's been so encouraging to me and I don't know how I could have processed all of this without him.

"Go to counseling. Do your thing," Chris always told me, as if going to counseling is no big deal. And that's what I needed to hear from him because sometimes I have made counseling into a big deal. I need to be reminded that I am not the only one who needs counseling.

The hardest part for Chris was feeling that he didn't know what to do with me because I was so emotionally crazy. Everything I was thinking was so abnormal for me. I was not the same girl that he started dating. But he loved me where I was and he has continued to love me as I have grown and changed.

I've been learning what God wants me to do with my emotions and how to incorporate logic into the process. Chris has helped me with this. Logical thinking is not my strong point, but Chris is all about logic, so he helps me incorporate it into my thinking.

Going through something so traumatic early on in our marriage has given us a different perspective on marriage, too. Chris has always said that we are a team and we do things together. He has always played sports so that analogy works for him. When I am struggling, it isn't just me who is struggling, but both of us together, because we're a team.

"Yes," he'll say. "You are having a bad day, but I'm here by your side. We'll do this together."

Chris has been so good and gracious with me. We've had an amazing few years of marriage. As difficult as this whole process has been, I wouldn't take anything back. I thought that my inability to deal with my emotions on my own could be more of a problem in our relationship than it has been and that made me afraid of letting Chris know the depth of my emotions. I shouldn't have sold him short. He has risen to the challenge and has held my hand every step of the way.

He doesn't push me. He wants to fix things, because he feels helpless and he wants to be able to do something about it, but sometimes there's nothing we can do but trust God together. There's no formula for us to follow.

I wonder sometimes what my life would have been like if Chris had not been on the plane that day. Had I been on the plane by myself, how would he understand why I'm struggling? It was a blessing at the time that I had someone by my side as we were crashing and it has continued to be a blessing that he knows exactly what I went through because he lived it, too.

I don't think that I was any more spiritual that day than I am today. I don't think I was any more in tune with God or that there was some special thing that I had to do that day in order to make everything turn out all right for me. I do believe that God wants us to seek Him every day, regardless of what we are going through.

At times, I can still be irrational. I'll be the first one to admit it and Chris will be right with me. But it's all right. For me every little thing gets multiplied by a thousand compared to other people. I can't help how I feel, but I *can* take charge of my reactions.

When we crashed, it wasn't a wakeup call for me the way it might have been for other people. It wasn't for Chris, either. It didn't feel like we needed to get our lives in order afterward, because we really had our priorities straight before. Our priorities were already in place. The crash just re-solidified them.

At any time, Chris could have said, "It's been a long time. Get over it." He could have grown impatient, but instead he was always trying his best to understand why I was feeling these things because I am on his "team." With a team mentality, you don't leave a player behind. You figure it out; you work together and you game-plan for the future.

For our marriage, the crash has been a blessing in disguise. It has been eye-opening to experience how we both struggle when we struggle as individuals. This has greatly shaped our marriage. We know that we are building the foundation of our marriage as we struggle and have adversity and ultimately overcome it. It has been a healthy dose of reality. We will never think, "Life is so dreamy and my spouse is everything I've ever wanted." We understand clearly who each other is and who God is. Those insights are invaluable.

34

My Future

Two things happen to me when I try to control my life. First, I get stuck in one specific part of a situation. Instead of seeing how this little piece is part of a beautiful whole, I fixate on the tiny piece because I don't understand how this piece could be good or beneficial for me. The flip side of this is that sometimes I have an idea of what the whole picture should look like, but I don't understand how this piece fits in.

I have come to realize that control is an illusion and I could make myself crazy grasping for it. When I try to control everything around me I miss out on fun, peace and joy. I become fearful and this becomes a vicious cycle. But God sees how it all fits together. God cares about the parts as much as the whole. God is in the details.

Coping with the unknown and struggling with the fear of not knowing when I'm going to die made me always try to plan ahead. I found the future scary and foreign and unknown. I will never understand the whole picture and I know that I am not meant to, but it was still hard for me. I wanted to know how everything would fit together. I would see people who were struggling and I wanted to make sense of it, but I had to learn to be OK with not knowing and not understanding.

In Romans 8:28 we read, "We know that in all things God works for the good of those who love him, who have been called according to his purpose." At some time during this process I began asking myself, what is "the good"? In my experience, sometimes good doesn't feel good or seem good. But the very next verse, verse 29, tells us that "the good" is to be conformed to Jesus' image, to be made in his likeness. Therefore, even though the journey has been difficult and not one that I would like to classify as "good" necessarily, it will be worth it if at the end I look more like Jesus.

At the beginning of this healing process, if someone had asked me my goal I probably would have said, *I want to feel normal again.* After I gained a little more perspective, I would have to change that to, *I don't know if there is such a thing as normal for me anymore.* My life was forever changed and my new "normal" is ever-changing. This is the new reality of my life. My life didn't stop when our plane went down, but neither did it start again right away. It took some time for me to start living again, and I am still a work in progress.

I continued to worry way more than I should. I worried about having children. I wanted to have a family with Chris, but fear suffocated me when I considered the amount of pain they could experience. And that caused more fear because I didn't want to live in fear if I had children. I didn't want to project that onto my kids.

I wanted to become a more whole me, whatever that actually meant. I felt that pieces of me had been missing since the crash and that the cracks that they left were only slowly starting to fill in again. I knew that there would be other traumatic events in my life and I that I couldn't sit around, holding my breath, waiting for them to happen. I needed to keep working through this so there wouldn't be compounded trauma. I needed to trust that Jesus would give me the necessary tools to go through whatever the future holds in His perfect timing even if it meant I would feel out of control for a while.

Someone in my family once said, "If you would have died, we wouldn't have questioned God. We would have been so heartbroken, but we wouldn't have thought any less of His love and protection for you. We wouldn't have questioned His love for you if you had died." That was hard for me to hear at first because it felt a little cold and heartless. I don't know if I would have thought the same way if the roles were reversed. It would be really hard for me not to ask "Why?"

I kept struggling with the question of "why." Why did God choose us that day to survive? Why were we on a plane where everyone survived and not on one where everyone died? Why did he spare us? For what purpose?

I don't think that I will be able to answer those questions until the end of my life when I look back and see what kind of impact I have had. I know that all life is valuable and that the lives of the people on Flight 1549 weren't more important than the lives of the people on other planes that have crashed. I don't think that I am better than anyone else, but I do believe that God saved us for a purpose.

And I believe that part of that purpose is telling my story.

God's wisdom and power allow Him to bring good out of evil. We accept this as truth. We cling to it during hard times. However, the good He brings is often different from what we envisioned. And therein lies the struggle. It has been difficult for me: How do I change my focus to being conformed to Jesus's image and not focusing on achieving a "good" and happy life? I haven't arrived yet. But each day I hope and pray that I am becoming more like Christ.

My goal will not be to have an easy life free from adversity and pain. It will be being *conformed*, as it says in the book of Romans, "...to be conformed to the image of his Son" (Romans 8:29). If you stop and think about it, you realize that most godly character can only be developed through adversity, when we are confronted with situations that require sacrificial love. God in his infinite wisdom knows exactly what we need and when and how to bring it. He is the perfect teacher and coach. And God never over-trains us by allowing too much adversity.

I don't want to go back to being "Old Karin." I can appreciate who she was because she laid the foundation for who I am today, but I don't want to go back to her. God has me on this path for a reason and all of these experiences are shaping me. I am becoming more of who I was meant to be. I hope I am becoming more like Jesus.

I want to be better. I want to be a better version of me, a better wife, a better daughter, a better friend. And I want to be healthy. To me, being healthy simply means not being so consumed by my anxieties and fears. I had no energy that first year after we were married. I could barely function because I was working through my emotions. I had nothing to give to anyone and even though I'm a relational person, I had no emotional or relationship energy to give to people. Being better means having more energy to give to people and support them in their journeys. I may not be there yet, but that is OK.

I'm never going to fully know who I am until I'm with God, but I am getting closer. I've never questioned whether I believe in God or not or whether He loves me. I just questioned whether God will sustain me through life's difficulties many times along this journey. I feel confident now that He will.

In his book, *Man's Search for Meaning*, Viktor Frankl speaks about our reactions to abnormal situations. He writes about Nazis during World War II, a topic much more serious and horrendous than my experience, but I found comfort in his words. My reaction to being in a plane crash was not normal to my mind, but once I realized how abnormal the very act of being in a plane crash was, I could release my desire to be "normal" and I could put forth the energy and concentration needed to begin the healing process.

Before the crash, I thought I was the best planner, the one who knew best what would be good and helpful for my life, what would benefit me the most. God has shown me through the crash that I am not the best planner—He is. All along, He was planning for my healing. He was planning for me to be conformed to the image of Jesus. As I let Him work in me to bring me to a place of healing, even though it took a long time, I have found a more complete healing than I could have planned for myself.

I am not there yet. I will always struggle with questions about the crash, but it is not my job to know everything. It is my job to trust in God's perfect plan and timing. It is my job to live.

I was faced with two options: to allow the tidal wave of emotions in the aftermath of the crash to define me and overpower me, or to sift through the ocean of emotions and learn how to cope and heal. I could stay where I was and keep sinking deeper and deeper into fear and anxiety or I could move on and swim.

I chose to swim.

35

A New Life

I was sitting with Chris in the hospital, watching my sister pace the halls in full-fledged labor. Tears streamed down my face as I watched her. She was being so strong in the midst of all the pain. Suddenly it hit me: God has made women to have babies. He has created our bodies to create and sustain life and He doesn't make mistakes. It seems so obvious, but this was the first time that I had really realized how present God is in the process of childbirth, just as He is in every process. Just as He was when we were crashing and when I was struggling and when I was figuring out how to live my life in a way that honored Him.

In that moment, my worries began to disappear and my fears about bringing children into the world began to lessen. I had looked up to my sister my entire life. I had wanted to be just like her. And there in the hospital, watching her struggle to give birth, I realized that I really did want to be just like her and that included trusting that God would give me all the tools I would need to be a good mother.

In 2011, Chris and I got an amazing opportunity to fly to Paris for two weeks for his job. While I was excited about the opportunity, I also felt considerable, understandable, dread. Committing to a fifteen-hour flight to Paris took more courage on my part than it would take for most people, but it was the chance of a lifetime and I didn't want to miss it. Although I considered not going several times, something in me assured me that we would be fine.

God's grace and provision were evident during the entire process of planning for the trip. We just happened to meet our captain during the first leg of our trip, which took us from Colorado to Washington, D.C. I told her our experience and she assured us that she would communicate about any turbulence or any other problems we might encounter on our flight. We were also blessed with an upgrade to business class, which made the flight much more endurable for us both—for me, because it didn't resemble our seats on Flight 1549, and for Chris, because his wife resembled a normal passenger for once.

When we told people that we were flying to Paris, many of them suggested I take a sleep aid or some other kind of medication to help me with the flight, but I decided not to. I wanted to face this fear head-on and to know that I survived without the help of drugs. It would be the first time that I had flown without some kind of medication to ease my stress since the crash, so it would be a big milestone for me.

I knew that it was God's provision that was allowing us to travel to Paris together and I tried my best to remain in a state of faith and gratitude and to block out my fears. I told myself: *The trip to Paris will be everything I hope for and more.*

It is on the flight to Paris that I would travel like a normal passenger for the first time since the crash.

It is in France that I would reconnect with my husband and begin to feel like myself again.

It is in Paris that we would conceive our first child, a daughter whose name means pure bright light.

Afterword

But you, Lord, are a shield about me, my glory, the
One who lifts my head high. I call out to the Lord,
and he answers me from his holy mountain. I lie
down and sleep; I wake again, because the Lord
sustains me. I will not fear. . . .

Psalm 3:3–6

In the summer of 2016 we had recently moved to Texas and
at Christmas we were planning to make our first visit home
to Colorado. After five months away from family, I was very
homesick.

I had asked Chris, if the ticket price wasn't too steep, how he
would feel about heading to Colorado to surprise our parents for
Thanksgiving. We started researching flights and everything fell
into place over the course of two days. Both his sister and mine
knew the plan and were excited to help us surprise our families.
I began packing our bags right away. I couldn't believe that in
just a few short days we would be flying home to Colorado! This
kind of surprise was something I had never done before. Not
only did I need to see my family, but I knew our families were
missing us as well and they would be so grateful to have all four
of us home. (Yes, we were now a family of four. Besides Elaina,
we had a baby son, Clark.)

I had flown many times since January 15, 2009, with the
help of coping techniques. Some helped to ease my anxiety, but

nothing had gotten rid of it completely. Every time, I would wake up after a restless night's sleep, my hands tingling, feeling like I needed to throw up, with my mind racing with thoughts about the plane's takeoff. In my counseling, I had learned the technique of envisioning, step by step, what I would do on the day of my flight; from leaving my home to landing safely in my destination. I worked on that, but I remember times of panic as I visualized what I should have hoped would be smooth travelling. So although I had taken more than a dozen flights since the crash, every time, I felt sick about flying.

On the morning of our Colorado flight, I woke up with so much excitement that all I could envision was the joy and thrill on our family members' faces when they saw our little family. Much to my amazement, my excitement was so big that it actually overpowered my anxieties. I awoke with no anxiety, no numb hands, no upset stomach. Being a mother of two children (with another on the way) helped immensely as I had little room for my own thoughts and worries. I had a busy morning ahead and the suspense of this surprise was growing!

We left for the airport and Chris prayed for the day to be safe, peaceful and filled with ease. We arrived at the parking lot and shuttle service and things began to move smoothly beyond my anticipation. My kids were happy and listening well, our luggage situation, which usually is hectic, was calm and the day continued to go smoothly as we reached our gate. I intermittently remembered to check myself for signs of anxiety and I was truly shocked at how peaceful I felt. I was not laboring to calm myself or my emotions. They were just calm.

We boarded our flight, spent most of the time situating the kids and began to taxi to take off. I was sitting with the kids and across the aisle was my husband—my rock. He was so calm. He smiled at me.

"How are you doing?" he asked, well aware of how flying had impacted me in the past.

"Surprisingly well," I said.

All these calm emotions were so new, so foreign. The kids were so excited too. I had always worked to hide from them my anxiety during flights so they would not pick up undue stress. I wanted them to love traveling and flying. But this day, I did not have to hide anything. I was actually able to relax and join them in their anticipation of returning to Colorado.

As we took off I felt a familiar, unwelcome rush come over me. I started to think, *This is so uncomfortable. This is hard.* An overwhelming sense of apprehension almost swept me away. However, the feeling had to be quickly pushed aside because my son needed my attention. I didn't have time to sit and worry. I needed to be a mom—I had little ones who needed me and although I felt I was in a risky situation, flying, knowing that my children were relying on me helped me overcome my fears.

We made it safely to Colorado and the surprise was everything I had hoped for. Our parents were thrilled, shocked and overjoyed to see us.

* * *

One of the biggest blessings I have received since the crash has been time: Time with Chris, my family and my children. Time to process, time to heal and change. Time to confront my fears and anxieties about life, death and flying. A specific truth about God, which I'm sure I have known since I was young, has become a constant in my heart: God never changes! While I change, my situation changes, my thoughts, feelings and emotions change; God never changes. He is immutable. He is the same yesterday, today, tomorrow and forever.

A lot has changed in my life since our plane went down in 2009 and for that I am incredibly thankful. Chris and I have been married eight years. We have three beautiful children, Elaina, Clark and Henry. I have accomplished educational goals and spent time working in foster care and adoption. I have grown in ways that I could not have predicted or imagined, proving once again that God knows better than I ever will. I am still a planner, but in a healthier way.

I have been through so much and it has taken me a long time to get to a place of peace and health, but I'm OK with that. Even in the midst of working through the trauma I wanted to bless the season that I was in. I didn't want to rush the healing process because, honestly, I didn't even know what the end goal looked like. I still don't.

When I look back through this book that I started writing about six years ago and I read about this woman named Karin and the life she was living daily, I feel far removed from her emotions, feelings and thoughts. Yet I'm also deeply touched in my heart, because I lived it. It brings me to thankful tears.

God in his infinite wisdom knows exactly what we need and when and how to bring it. He is the perfect teacher and coach; he never "over trains" us by allowing too much adversity. Today, I know I'm in a deeper place of understanding God's provisional love and am more willing to surrender to *His* plan for my life. I can relinquish control, knowing that He is faithful. I can be confident even when I seem undone and afraid.

I now know how to be comfortable in the moment, how to be intentional about the process, how to allow my heart to experience every emotion, even the darkest ones, so that I can fully embrace the light. I bless the process. I welcome the difficulties.

As I have grown through these past several years, I have had ups and downs in my faith, my confidence as a person, my role as a wife and young mother. I have had to confront my beliefs on who God is and then look at my situation. While I needed time to address the trauma of the plane crash, I also needed to confront the beliefs I had about God; beliefs about His character, His Word, His work in my life and His sovereignty. Those beliefs directly impacted me and how I lived my daily life.

I can most assuredly tell you that it was only God's power that helped me, because in my own strength I never could have had what it would take to address the hand I had been dealt. I could never have talked myself through the mountain that confronted me. What I had within me was nothing. I didn't have the strength or the power to face the fears and anxieties that consumed me every day.

I had to believe the Scriptures such as Romans 8:28 about God working all things for good. I learned to hang on to the truth that He never leaves or forsakes His children (see Deuteronomy 32:6). He carried me, "for it is God who works in you to will and to act in order to fulfill his good purpose" (Philippians 2:13). I have the power of Christ in me to overcome hard things.

I have come and continue to come to a clearer, more correct knowledge of who God is and who I am in light of that truth. I know trials will come; I have a lot more life to live. One thing I know for sure, something I cling to mightily, is that God will always be the Rock on which I stand.

I won't sink. I can't sink. I have Jesus as my Savior and together we will swim.

Endnotes

1. Ann Spangler, *Praying the Names of God: A Daily Guide* (Grand Rapids: Zondervan, 2004), 53.

2. Hannah Anderson, *Made for More: An Invitation to Live in God's Image* (Chicago: Moody Publishers, 2014), chapter 10 epigraph.

3. Viktor E. Frankl, *Man's Search for Meaning* (Boston: Beacon, 1946), 38.

4. Frankl, 1.

5. C.S. Lewis, *Mere Christianity* (New York: HarperCollins, 2001), 189.